The Blackbird Academy Foundations

Pensado's Strive Education Series

The Blackbird Academy Foundations

Must-Know Audio and Recording Principles

KEVIN BECKA

Hal Leonard Books
An Imprint of Hal Leonard LLC

Published in 2017 by Hal Leonard Books
An Imprint of Hal Leonard LLC
7777 West Bluemound Road
Milwaukee, WI 53213

Trade Book Division Editorial Offices
33 Plymouth St., Montclair, NJ 07042

All photos and illustrations are from the author's collection except for the photos on pages 13, 14, 20, 25, 26 (top and middle), 27, and 28 (top and middle), which are from Adobe Stock, and those on pages 28 (bottom), 29, and 30, which are from Shutterstock.

Printed in the United States of America
Book design by Kristina Rolander

Library of Congress Cataloging-in-Publication Data

Names: Becka, Kevin, author. | Blackbird Academy, editor.
Title: The Blackbird Academy foundations : must-know audio and recording principles / Kevin Becka.
Other titles: Foundations
Description: Milwaukee, WI : Hal Leonard Books, an Imprint of Hal Leonard LLC, 2017. | Series: Pensado's strive education series
Identifiers: LCCN 2017041192 | ISBN 9781495069345
Subjects: LCSH: Sound--Recording and reproducing.
Classification: LCC TK7881.4 .B435 2017 | DDC 621.389/3--dc23
LC record available at https://lccn.loc.gov/2017041192

www.halleonardbooks.com

Contents

Introduction

The Blackbird Academy Foundations is created with the beginner to intermediate music maker in mind. Each course is based on the same workflow and developed in the same studios used to make hit records by Taylor Swift, Chris Stapleton, Jack White, James Bay, Hunter Hayes, Reliant K, Martina McBride, and more. This book covers the basics: signal flow, electrical levels in audio, cables and connectors, the digital audio workstation (DAW), converters, and plug-ins that make music loved by millions. You'll get an overview of the steps involved in making great, professional recordings, a knowledge of the terminology and tools involved, and an understanding of how the pieces all fit together, so that when you enter a recording studio, you'll be well oriented, and everything will make sense. No other book shows you more of what goes on behind the scenes in studios used by international recording artists, engineers, and producers.

The chapters are short, easily digestible lessons covering microphone types and placement, phase, balanced signals, gain staging, EQ and compression, serial and parallel processing, and the use of virtual instruments. You'll learn quickly and at your own pace through step-by-step infographics illustrating concepts used at the top levels of production.

The Blackbird Academy has trained some of the best new faces in recording and live sound engineering who now work at some of the top studios in the world, and tour with the biggest names in music. Be a part of the Blackbird experience and build your skills.

The Blackbird Academy Foundations

1

Understanding Recording Signal Flow

The Blackbird Academy Foundations is designed to improve your recording knowledge and skills. The first chapter, "Understanding Recording Signal Flow," lays out the framework for the entire book. In this chapter we'll walk through the basic building blocks of signal flow and look at how it works as a whole.

THE SOURCE

A great recording always starts with a great sound. Sources can range from acoustic instruments like guitar, drums, piano, voice, and percussion, to electronic amplified instruments like bass, electric guitar, and keyboards. No matter the source, it has to sound good to be good. While you can fix timing and add effects and EQ later in the process to improve a sound, it's always best to get it right before you push record. This means properly tuning the instruments, replacing strings and drum heads if necessary, and recording in isolated spaces away from other ambient noise. The source is the most important link in the signal chain. None of the following signal-flow steps can make a bad source sound great.

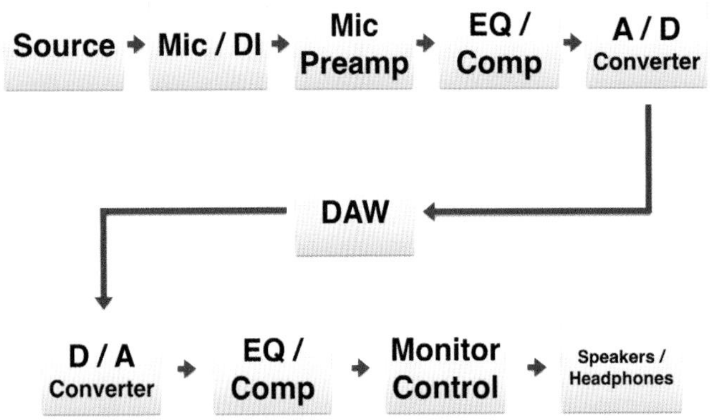

THE MICROPHONE

Microphones are used to record anything that makes a sound in the physical world, including acoustic instruments, percussion, vocals, and more. Mics come in many shapes and sizes, and range from simple, affordable models to more expensive units with more features. We'll explore mic placement techniques and choices later in the book.

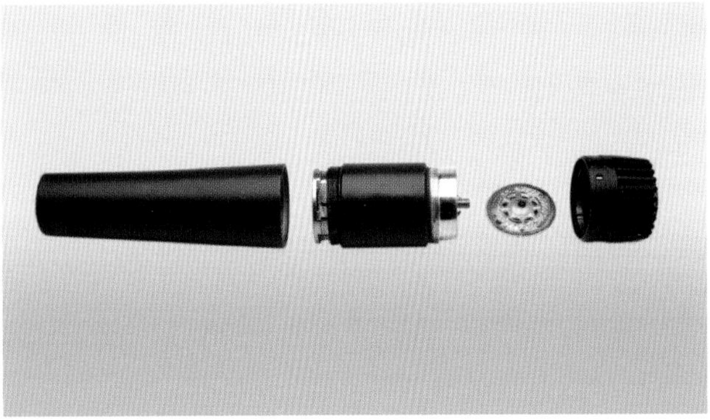

Common studio microphones fall into two basic categories: dynamic and condenser. Let's tackle dynamic mics first. They fall into two sub-categories: moving coil and ribbon. A moving coil mic works much like a speaker, except in reverse. The microphone's diaphragm reacts to acoustic energy from the source, which in turn pushes a wire coil across a fixed magnet. This creates an electrical signal at the mic's output.

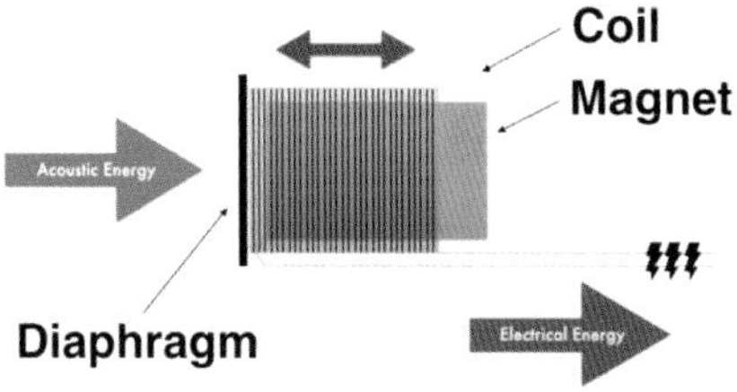

Dynamic Element (side view)

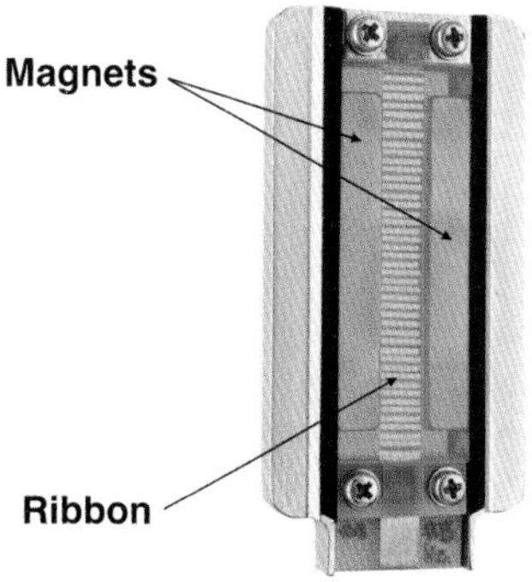

Royer R-121 Ribbon Element

A ribbon mic is also very simple, but instead of a diaphragm and coil, a ribbon mic has a thin, corrugated metal ribbon that moves across a fixed magnet when acoustic energy is introduced. Again, this creates an electrical signal at the ribbon mic's output.

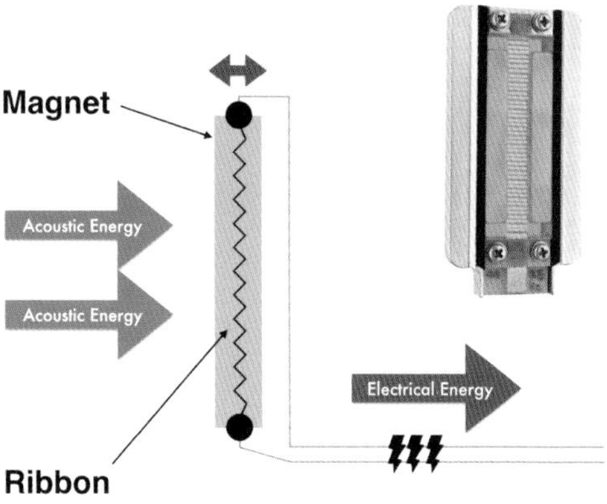

Ribbon Element (side view)

A condenser mic is more complex, using a thin membrane and a charged backplate to create a signal. Unlike simple dynamic mics, a condenser mic must be powered externally to operate. The microphone is the step in the signal flow chain at which acoustic energy is translated into electrical energy.

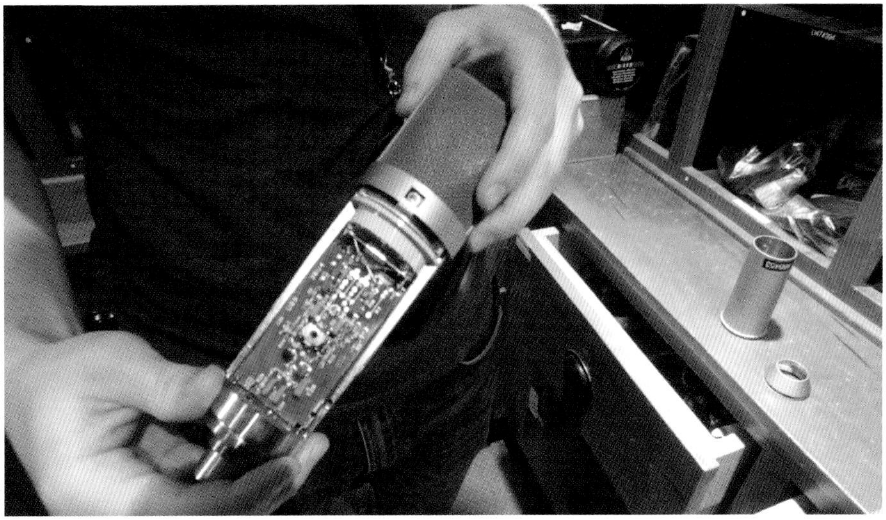

THE DIRECT BOX (DI)

A microphone works well when recording an instrument or voice that makes sound acoustically. But what about when recording electronic instruments that don't resonate and have a wired output? This is when you must use a DI box. DI stands for direct inject or direct input.

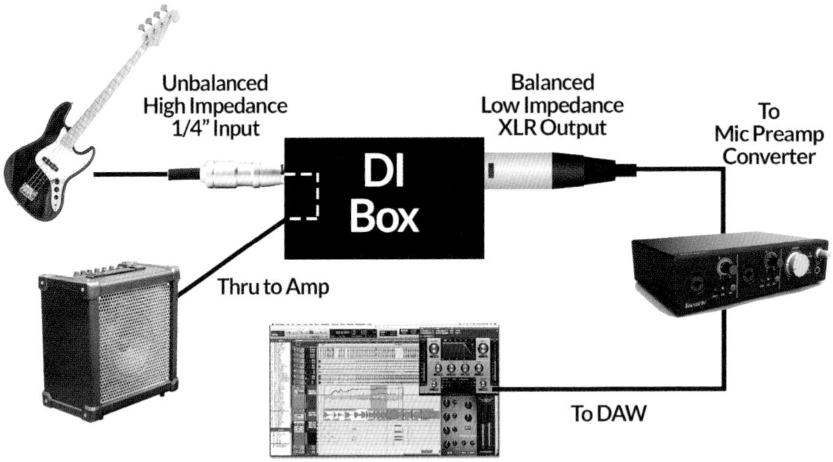

The DI box is an essential studio tool that acts as a bridge to the next step in the signal flow. It changes the unbalanced, high-impedance output of an instrument to a balanced, low-impedance signal preferred by professional studio gear. DI boxes can be purchased as a completed product ready to plug-and-play, or as a do-it-yourself kit. Because of the simple nature of a DI box, making your own is a great way to save money and affordably build your collection of studio gear.

THE MICROPHONE PREAMP

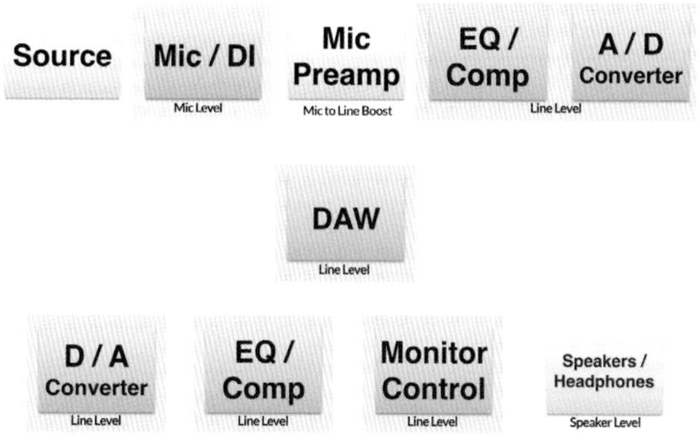

Before you can record a signal from a microphone or DI box, it must first be sent through a microphone preamp. A mic preamp boosts an audio signal from mic level to line level. The great majority of audio gear in the recording signal path between the microphone and speakers operates at line level. This includes consoles, processors, and other gear.

A preamp can be found on a console or purchased as a standalone unit. Some mic preamps come with a built-in DI. The input for the DI is usually found on the front of the unit and negates the need for a separate DI box. Using this feature allows you to record a guitar, bass, or other instrument by plugging directly into the preamp through its built-in DI input.

The microphone preamp plays a vital and early role in studio signal flow. A preamp boosts the signal from a microphone or DI box up to line level, which is the same level used by consoles, EQs, compressors, DAWs, and other gear along the signal flow chain.

ANALOG PROCESSING BEFORE RECORDING

There are two types of hardware-based processing that are commonly applied to a signal before recording. The first is called EQ, which stands for equalization. EQ allows you to boost or cut various frequency bands in the audible spectrum. Equalization is a common feature in both consumer and professional audio gear. For example, the bass and treble controls on your car radio are a type of EQ. In the studio, EQ can be found on a console or as a standalone unit. Typical uses for EQ include adding more low end to a bass or kick drum, and adding more high-frequency emphasis to cymbals or percussion.

The second type of processing sometimes used before recording is compression and limiting. Compression and limiting reduces the dynamic range of a signal, bringing the softest and the loudest parts closer together. Compression is often used on vocals to make quieter passages more audible while controlling the volume of the louder passages. Some consoles have compressors built in. Compression can also be applied by a standalone unit. The important thing to note here is that using a processor before recording writes the effect directly to the track and is permanent. We'll explore EQ and compression and how to use it later in the book.

A/D AND D/A CONVERTERS

Before an analog signal can be digitally recorded, it must be converted to a digital format using an A/D, or analog-to-digital converter. Once an analog signal is converted to digital, it can then be ported into a computer using USB, FireWire, Thunderbolt, or other interfaces.

An A/D converter can be either a standalone unit or built in to an audio interface with mic preamps, direct inputs, and other extra features. When the signal exits the digital recorder, once again it must be converted using a D/A or digital-to-analog converter. While converters can be purchased separately, most often they reside in the same box. It's important to remember that the DAW, or digital audio workstation, sits right in the middle of the analog-to-digital and digital-to-analog conversion process.

DIGITAL AUDIO WORKSTATION SOFTWARE

The digital audio workstation, or DAW, is the basis for all modern recording. Inside the DAW, you can mix, edit, and process the recorded signals in many different ways. Mixing inside the DAW mimics an analog console's features, including level control via faders, panning, aux sends, and the ability to use plug-ins for processing like EQ and compression. Plug-ins are add-on software programs used inside a DAW for signal processing and other manipulation such as vocal and instrument tuning. We'll be exploring the DAW and plug-ins in greater depth later in the book.

ANALOG PROCESSING AFTER RECORDING

Optionally, audio from the DAW can be processed after it has been recorded. This is a common workflow when mixing. At this point, EQ and compression can be applied by digital processors called plug-ins—used inside the DAW—or via analog hardware after D/A conversion. Like analog hardware, plug-in types are diverse and include many types of applications including time-based processors such as reverbs and delays.

It's important to note that this is a non-destructive process during playback. The files from the DAW will not be effected from this type of processing because it takes place after the signal has been recorded.

MONITOR CONTROL

Monitor control, whether it's on a console or a freestanding unit, gives you the ability to control speaker loudness, source selection, and monitor selection if you have more than one pair of speakers. More sophisticated and expensive units will offer talkback for use when recording, separate headphone outputs with dedicated volume controls, and possibly surround capabilities for monitoring in 5.1.

Some audio interfaces are a one-stop shop offering many of the steps along the signal chain, including monitor control, A/D and D/A conversion, microphone preamps, and DI inputs. No matter what type of studio you're in, monitor control is an essential stop along the signal's path, allowing you to tailor your listening experience optimally. It's the last stop before electrical energy is turned back into acoustic energy.

SPEAKERS AND HEADPHONES

The last stop in the signal chain before you hear the results of your work are the speakers or headphones. Monitors come in two basic types—passive and active. Passive monitors need a separate amplifier, while active monitors have their own amplifiers built in. Headphones come in closed- and open-back formats. Closed-back headphones are better for musician and studio use because they prevent the signal from leaking back into the microphone. Open-back headphones are sometimes preferred for mixing due to their more realistic tone. Because they're open to the outside, open-back headphones make the listening experience more like monitoring with speakers.

SIGNAL FLOW RECAP

Let's take a moment to recap what we've learned about recording signal flow.

It all starts with the source, which is captured with a microphone or DI box. Next, the signal is boosted to line level using the microphone preamp. At this point you can optionally EQ or compress your signal before it moves on to the analog-to-digital converter and DAW software. The trip back to the listener starts with the digital-to-analog converter, and possibly continues to other analog processing before moving into the monitor controller and ultimately the speakers or headphones for you to hear.

2

Electrical Levels in Audio Production

The Blackbird Academy Foundations is designed to build your music engineering and production skills. It's recommended that you read the chapters in their numbered sequence to avoid confusion as we move on to more advanced topics. The second chapter, "Electrical Levels in Audio Production," lays out the types of electrical signals that flow from, into, or through microphones, instruments, processors, consoles, and speakers.

WHAT IS A DECIBEL?

In audio production, the decibel is used to measure the operating level, intensity of sound, or electrical output produced by a piece of gear. It's represented by the symbol dB, and named after Alexander Graham Bell, the inventor of the telephone.

Decibels are confusing. Through the years, there have been many decibel scales created to measure audio electronics and voltage, including: dBm, dBu, dB capital V, dB lower case v, dB FS, dB SPL, dBA, dBB, dBC, dBTP, dBUV, and more.

The good news is there are only two decibel scales commonly used for audio gear: dBu and dBV. Pro audio gear, like you'd find in a professional recording studio, use

the +4dBu scale, referenced at 0 VU. This means when the output reaches 0 VU on an audio meter, the electrical output measures +4 dBu, which is 1.23 volts.
Consumer audio gear are measured on the -10dBV scale, with "V" meaning volt. This means when the signal reaches 0 VU, the electrical output measures -10 dBV, which is 316 millivolts. (mV is the symbol used to represent a millivolt. One millivolt is 1 / 1,000th of a Volt.)

Because dBu and dBV are referenced to different voltages at 0 VU, you cannot freely add or subtract the values to compare the differences. The key to doing the math between dB scales is to translate them to the same voltage scale. For example, we know that +4 dBu = 1.23 volts. On the dBV scale, 1.23 volts = 1.79 dBV.

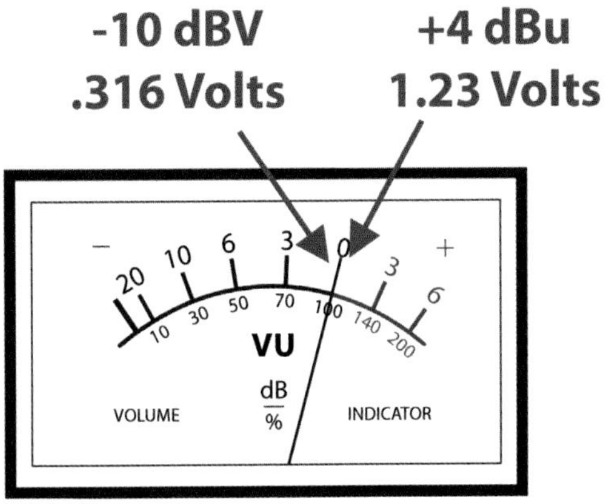

CONSUMER VS. PRO AUDIO GEAR

Audio gear falls into two categories: professional and consumer. What differentiates the two in the broad sense is the intended use. Professional gear is used in recording studios and other production environments for creating music and other content for release to the public. Consumer audio gear, such as computers, TVs, and car stereos, are for consuming content. In a technical sense, the biggest difference between pro and consumer gear is the input/output level and whether these inputs/outputs are balanced or unbalanced. We'll explore balanced connections in more depth in a future chapter, but for now, it's important to know the basic differences between the cables and connectors used for each type.

XLR and TRS connectors are used for balanced connections. RCA and TS connectors are used for unbalanced connections.

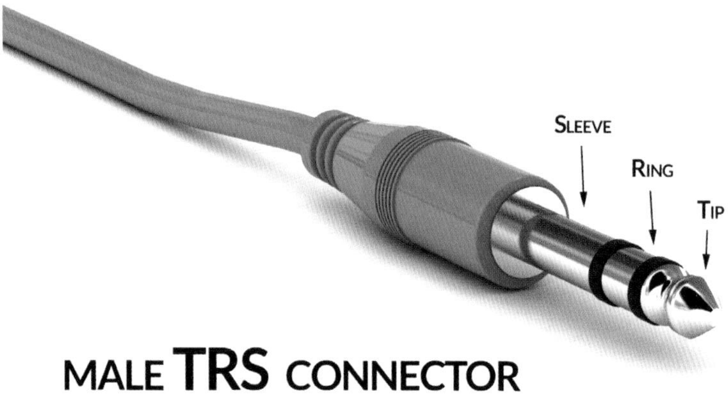

A balanced connection requires three separate signal paths in the connector and cable to operate. For example, in the above photos of XLR and TRS connectors, you can see three isolated parts, each carrying a separate signal. In the XLR connector, the parts are called pins. In the TRS connector, they are called tip, ring, and sleeve. In an unbalanced connector, like an RCA or TS connector, there are only two parts: signal and ground.

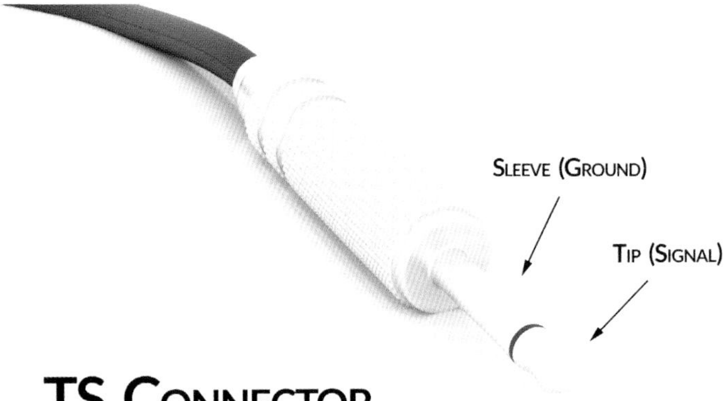

TS Connector

Pro audio gear typically uses balanced connections, and is manufactured for professional use in recording, live sound, broadcast, and post-production environments. For this reason, it generally costs more than consumer audio gear. Some examples of pro audio gear would be microphones, compressors and EQs, consoles, studio monitors, and various A/D and D/A converters. Although consumer audio gear may be used in recording and audio production, it is not expressly designed for that purpose. For example, guitars, basses, amplifiers, guitar pedals, and electronic keyboards are found on many recordings, but were first created for general use in clubs, churches, and other venues. Other types of consumer products with audio outputs include TVs, computers, smartphones, car radios, sound docks, and other portable devices.

In the next sections of this chapter, we'll break down the four common electrical levels found in audio production. They fall into four categories: mic, line, instrument, and speaker.

MIC LEVEL

As we learned in the first chapter of the *Foundations*, a microphone changes acoustic energy into electrical energy. The electrical output level of a microphone is very weak, so weak in fact, that its output is measured in millivolts, noted by the symbol mV. Ribbon, moving coil, and condenser microphones all have different output levels. For example, at 117 decibels input, the level of sound you'd hear at a loud rock concert, a Royer R-121 has a 50 millivolt output; a Shure SM57 has a 22.4 millivolt output; and a Neumann condenser microphone has a 390 millivolt output. Because a microphone's level is weak, it must be boosted using a microphone preamp. The preamp accepts a mic level input, which is boosted to line level at the output. Line level is the optimal operating level of most professional audio gear.

LINE LEVEL

Once an audio signal is boosted to professional line level, it can be freely routed to other pro audio gear such as compressors, EQs, converters, consoles, and the inputs of powered speakers. It's important to remember that most of an audio signal's lifetime in the signal chain is spent at line level and is +4dBu referenced at 0 VU output. Although many audio devices offer faders and potentiometers that effect the overall output gain, they are still considered to operate at line level.

A potentiometer is called a pot for short and is found on many consumer and pro audio devices. A pot can be used for many purposes such as changing frequencies on an EQ, altering tone like bass and treble, and panning signal left, right, and center on a mixer. If you see the words "gain" or "output" labeled on a pot, it is most likely used for volume control.

INSTRUMENT LEVEL

Instruments such as guitars, basses, guitar pedals, and electronic keyboards are consumer audio devices. They are referenced at -10dBV, have unbalanced outputs, and are high impedance. These three basic characteristics make them incompatible with pro audio gear. However, with the right interfaces and cabling, it's easy to integrate them into a recording studio workflow. First let's demystify impedance.

Impedance is the measurement of resistance that "impedes" or obstructs electric current flowing from one device to another. Think of electrical flow like water through a pipe. If you try to push a large amount of water through a small pipe, the water will spill over the edges—the pipe impedes the flow of water. It's easier for current to flow from one point to another when the impedance is matched between the two systems, or the source impedance is lower than the destination impedance. For this reason, you can't directly patch a high impedance guitar output into a lower impedance mic preamp input—it must be matched using a DI box. DI boxes change an unbalanced, high impedance signal, to a balanced, low impedance signal that can be patched directly into a mic preamp. Some preamps have DI functionality built in that negates the need for an external box. In this case, you can plug an instrument directly into the mic preamp.

SPEAKER LEVEL

Once the signal has been recorded and it's time to hear your work, it must be sent through another transducer—a speaker or set of headphones—to send the signal through air, once again on the way to our ears. Line level is much too weak to move heavy speaker components, so the signal must be boosted to speaker level using a power amp. A power amp can be integrated into the speaker itself, or it can be a separate unit that is then patched into the speaker's input. An *active* speaker has its own power amp, often inside the enclosure. A *passive* speaker requires a separate power amp.

Speaker power is measured in watts, named after Scottish engineer James Watt. The gain, or volume of the speaker, is managed by a volume pot found on a console, audio interface, or separate monitor controller. This volume control lives between the line level output of the mixer and the input of the speaker's amplifier.

ELECTRICAL LEVEL RECAP

Let's recap what we've learned about the electrical levels in audio production.

The decibel is used to measure the operating level, intensity of sound, or electrical output produced by a piece of gear. Pro audio gear is measured at +4dBu referenced at 0 VU output, which is 1.23 volts, while consumer audio gear is measured at -10dBV, which is referenced at 316mV (or millivolts). There are four common electrical levels found in audio production: mic, line, instrument, and speaker.

3

Cables and Connectors

Cables and connectors provide the pathways for audio signals to flow throughout the studio. Great connections can make a creative difference in the recording process by maintaining the quality of the source, whether it's a voice, guitar, bass, piano, drums or whatever else you're recording. When the talent hears a quality recording, it inspires them to play and sing their best. Whether you make your cables yourself, or buy them commercially, it's important that your connections are made using the best quality components.

WHAT'S ON YOUR CABLE?

There are many different types of cables and connectors used in audio recording. Signals carried on these cables can be balanced, unbalanced, high impedance, low impedance, analog, digital, one channel, or many channels. For example, a 120-pin Elco connector can carry forty separate balanced analog signals down the same group of cables to a common connector. A multi-channel analog cable that carries many signals is called a snake and can terminate to all kinds of different connections, such as XLR, DB25, TRS, Elco, and more.

120-pin ELCO connector can carry up to 40, balanced, analog audio signals

Digital audio connections take the multi-channel concept even further, while using far less cable. For example, Roland's REAC protocol can send power, plus forty channels of audio in each direction, while Audinate's Dante protocol allows hundreds of bi-directional channels of audio to be distributed over long distances. Both systems use inexpensive and readily available Cat-5e or Cat-6 network cable. Thunderbolt-enabled interfaces can port many channels of audio and video over long distances to a computer, monitor, and other devices. An ADAT lightpipe cable, also called TOSLINK, can carry up to eight channels of audio to and from other compatible gear. Digital audio has made getting signals from here to there much easier and affordable in studio and live sound applications.

Roland Ethernet Audio Communication (REAC)

40 channels of audio plus power

Before we get into more details on cables and connections, let's read about the types of signals traveling over the many cables found in a recording studio. As we learned in the first chapter of this book, it's important that your source be in the best possible shape to assure great results. It's also important to know the type of signal you're sending along a cable in order to avoid bad-sounding recordings and possible damage to your gear. For example, never plug a high-impedance source into a low-impedance input.

A high-impedance source, such as a guitar or bass, must first be run through a DI box, which changes an unbalanced, high-impedance input into a balanced, low-impedance output. Once the impedance is matched, or the source has a lower impedance than the next step in the signal chain, then you're assured your signal will be sounding great.

While an impedance mismatch won't damage your gear, a speaker level signal can cause damage if it's plugged into the wrong input. Never run a speaker level signal into anything but a speaker or a device specifically made to handle a speaker level input. For example, you should never run a speaker output of a guitar or bass amp head into a *standard* DI box, guitar amp, or input of an audio interface. The high wattage supplied by the output of a power amplifier will, without a doubt, fry your gear if you plug it into a line or mic level input.

BALANCED AND UNBALANCED SIGNALS

We learned in the last chapter that a mic level signal is measured in millivolts, which is very weak. For this reason, when the signal is sent along a cable, it is susceptible to noise caused by radio frequency interference, called RFI, and electro magnetic interference, called EMI. A standard mic cable greatly reduces this noise by using three separate methods for noise reduction, one of which is over one hundred years old.

A balanced cable consists of three conductors, two of which are a twisted pair that carries the audio. This technique of twisting pairs to reduce RFI and EMI was invented in 1881 by the Bell Telephone Company for use in telephone lines. The third conductor in the cable is the ground, or shield wire, which works to eliminate hum and the danger of electric shock.

But the primary way a balanced line reduces noise is by carrying "hot" and "cold" versions of the audio signal, each on a separate wire within the cable. The hot version of the signal has a positive polarity, and the cold version has a negative polarity. This means for every plus voltage, there is an equal and opposite minus voltage traveling down the cable. During the journey, any noise that hitches a ride on the cable is at a positive voltage on *both* wires, which brings us to the magic. A differential amplifier at the end of the signal path amplifies the hot and cold signals putting them back into polarity, while at the same time putting the noise out of polarity with itself. From there it's simple math—equal and opposite numbers added together equal zero—meaning the noise is gone. Genius!

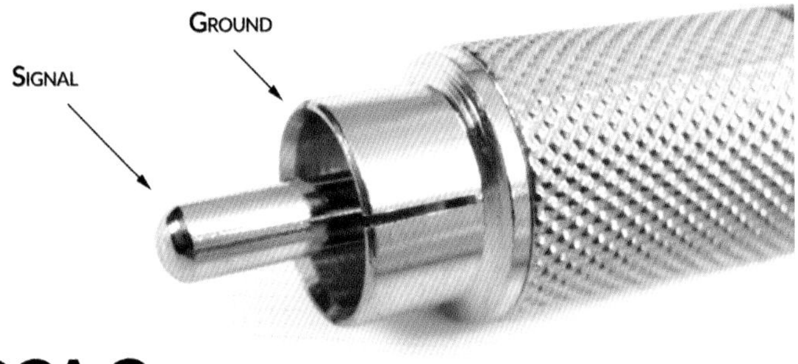

RCA CONNECTOR

Unbalanced lines like ¼" instrument and RCA cables are much simpler, using only one conductor for audio and another for ground. Because there are no twisted pairs, or hot and cold signals, an unbalanced line is susceptible to noise over long runs. The rules are simple: use balanced lines for pro audio recording where signals travel over long distances, but for instruments and consumer audio applications over short distances, unbalanced lines are the best way to go.

ANALOG AND DIGITAL AUDIO CABLES

Analog audio signals in a recording studio fall into four categories: mic level, line level, instrument level, and speaker level. While mic and line level signals may use the same types of cables, instrument and speaker level signals use different types.

When it comes to digital audio, there are a completely different set of cables, connectors, and requirements. To clear up any confusion, here is a quick guide to the common cables used for analog and digital audio.

- Microphone level and balanced +4dB line level signals use XLR, TRS, TT, and many other types of balanced cables and snakes. The key requirement is that the cable has three conductors for carrying hot, cold, and ground.
- Unbalanced, –10dBV consumer level signals use mono RCA cables often found on home stereos and TVs, and ⅛" stereo plugs as you would find on earbuds. The stereo ⅛" plug looks very much like a balanced TRS cable, however instead of carrying hot, cold, and ground, it carries left, right, and ground, and is unbalanced.

- Unbalanced instrument level signals, like those from a guitar, guitar pedal, bass and electronic keyboard, use ¼" TS instrument cables.
- Speaker level signals use ¼" unshielded speaker cables, Speakon cables, RCA, and BNC cables and connectors. While a ¼" speaker cable looks like a ¼" instrument cable, it is different in that there is no shielding or grounding against noise because of the high voltage levels carried by the cable. It's important to know the difference between speaker and instrument cables, and use each for its intended application for the best results.
- Digital cables for professional audio include 110-ohm AES/EBU XLR cables and 75-ohm RCA cables. These cables are more expensive than standard XLR and RCA cables and may be purposed for analog use, but regular XLR and RCA cables are not recommended for digital use. Other cables used for digital audio include BNC, Cat-5e and Cat-6 Ethernet, fiber optic, TOSLINK, FireWire 400 and 800, USB, Thunderbolt, and USB Type-C. The USB Type-C can be used for both power and USB 3.1 data as on the latest Apple computers. USB 3.1's data transfer rate is 10 gigabits per second, which is twice as fast as USB 3.0 and the same speed as Thunderbolt.

BITS, BYTES, AND MORE

Digital audio is the most common format for recording and storing sound in the modern studio. We'll be exploring how digital audio is created and recorded in a future chapter, but for now, let's read about the speed and storage of digital sound and what exactly is traveling on a digital cable.

The word *bandwidth* refers to the transfer rate, or speed of digital data over a network. For example, the internet bandwidth into the average U.S. home is roughly 35 megabits per second. But what does this mean? What's a bit, and what's a byte?

Bits and bytes are just some of the terms used to describe units of digital data. It all starts with the bit. Think of a bit like a two-way switch: it's either on or off. A byte is a collection of 8 bits, which is like eight light switches, each of which can be set to 1 or 0. A byte can express 256 possible combinations, which is okay for a small amount of data, such as characters on a computer keyboard, but there is a need to express larger amounts of data when storing the huge files created for digital audio and other applications.

After the bit comes the byte. There's the kilobyte, megabyte, gigabyte, terabyte, petabyte, exabyte, zettabyte, and lastly the yottabyte. The math is straightforward. A kilobyte is 1,024 bytes, a megabyte is 1,024 kilobytes, a gigabyte is 1,024 megabytes and so on. So you *could* say that a 1 terabyte hard drive has 1,024 gigabytes of storage. By the way, it is predicted that by the year 2025, civilization will have generated 163 zettabytes of information.

Bits and bytes can both represent data speed, while bytes alone are used to describe data storage. For example, earlier we said the internet speed into in the average US home is roughly 35 megabits per second. The shortcut for 35 megabits per second is the number 35 followed by capital M, lowercase b, lowercase p, lowercase s. The shortcut for mega*bytes* per second would be expressed with capital M, capital B, lowercase p, lowercase s. The general rule is: lowercase b for bits, and capital B for bytes.

When it comes to data transfer rates, cables are just the highways for the data. The transfer *format* is where the speed happens. Here are the numbers: FireWire 400 was introduced by Apple in the late 90s and operates at 400 megabits per second, while the second-generation FireWire 800 is twice as fast. The most common digital cable and format is USB, which was developed by a group of seven companies and released in 1996 at a speed of 12 megabits per second. USB 2.0 followed at 480 megabits per second, then USB 3.0 at 5 gigabits per second. The latest is USB 3.1, also called SuperSpeed USB, which is 10 gigabits per second. Apple's Thunderbolt format is also 10 gigabits per second.

What's the advantage of all this speed? Faster data speed between your digital audio software and your hard drive, along with a fast processor and plenty of RAM, will result in faster and smoother operation, leaving plenty of horsepower for virtual instruments and other processing.

KEEPING IT NEAT

Cables are a major investment in your studio, so it's important to store them properly. Winding the cable over your elbow in continuous loops will introduce continuous twists and cause knots, which will wear down the cable over time and make them hard to work with. The correct way to wind any cable is in an over-under method. Take the cable in one hand, grab the cable with your thumb up, and make a loop about the size of your head. Then with your thumb pointing down, make a reverse loop that lays on top of the first loop. Repeat this process until the cable is completely wound. Cables wound this way will be easier to unwind without any knots. It's also a good practice to refrain from throwing the cable out on the floor when you unwind it, to avoid damaging the XLR connectors.

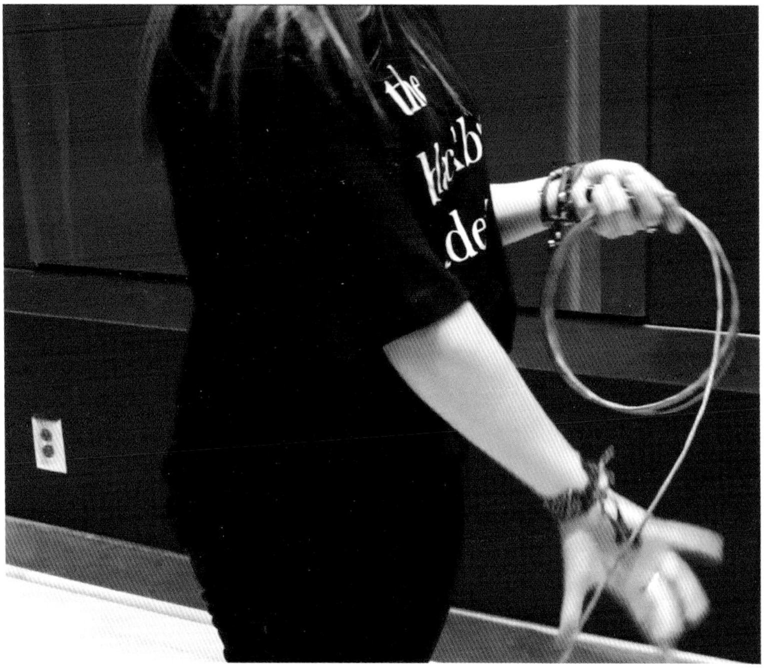

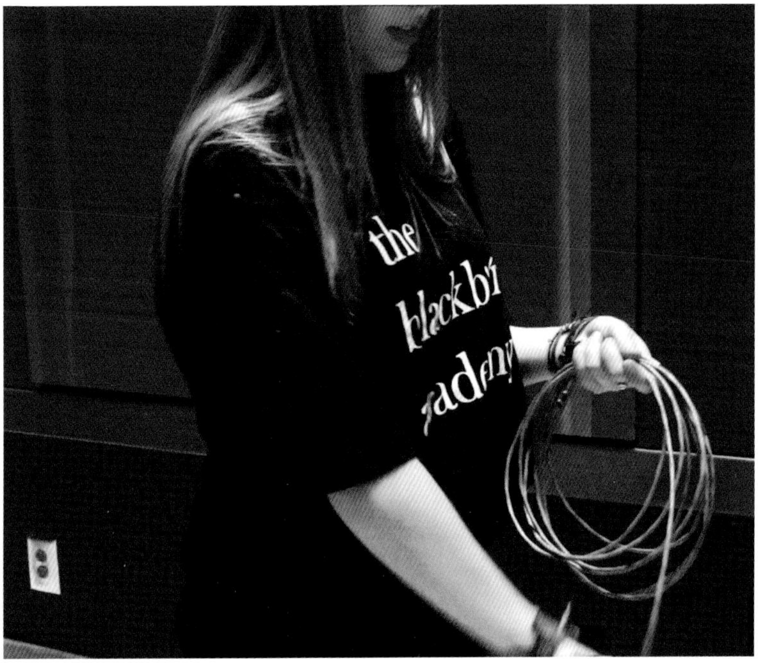

When setting up microphones in the studio, lay excess cable at the bottom of each mic stand. This will make it easier to extend the boom arm and freely move the mic stand for precise placement. Once all your cables are laid out, go around the room and tidy up any stray loops that may cause someone to trip. Use gaffer's tape to tack down any runs of cable in high traffic areas. Also be careful not to roll any heavy cases over your cables to avoid crimping or damaging them. When the talent arrives, it's inspiring to see well thought-out and neatly-arrayed cables. Studio aesthetics can affect the creative side of recording: when the studio looks neat, the talent will respect the fact that you care and it will reflect in their performance.

CABLES AND CONNECTORS RECAP

Let's recap some of the important concepts we've learned.

A multi-channel analog cable that carries many signals is called a snake and can terminate to all kinds of different connections like XLR, DB25, TRS, Elco, and more. Microphone level and balanced +4dB line level signals use XLR, TRS, TT, and many other types of balanced cables and snakes.

A bit is like a two-way switch with on and off representing a 1 or a 0. A byte is a collection of 8 bits, which is like eight light switches, each of which can be set to 1 or 0. There are 256 combinations of 1s and 0s in a byte. The general rule when writing out bits and bytes is: lowercase b for bits, and capital B for bytes. A kilobyte is 1,024 bytes, a megabyte is 1,024 kilobytes, and so on. Digital cables have nothing to do with speed, they just carry various digital formats, the speed of which has increased steadily over the years.

XLR

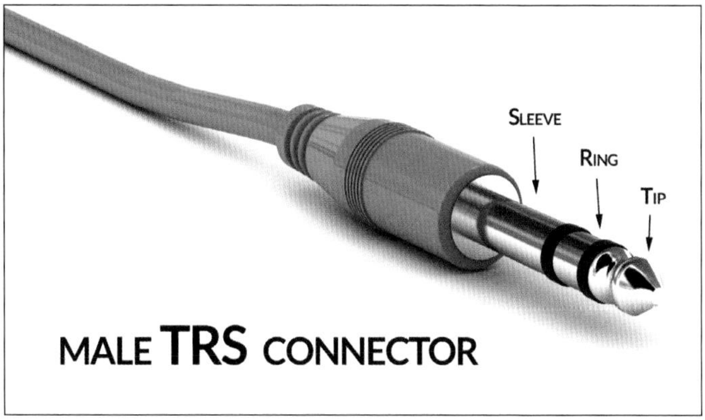

TRS

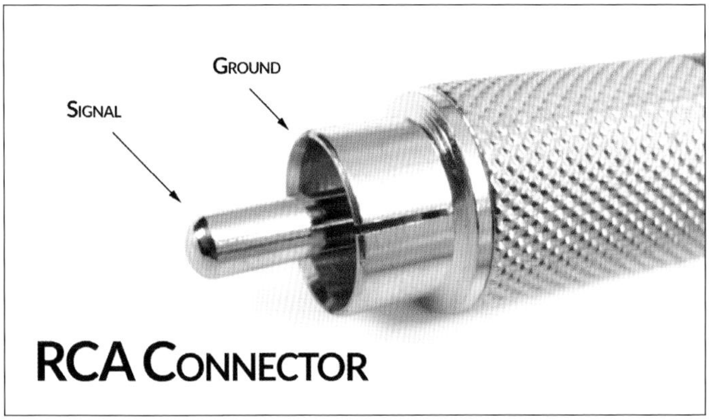
Ground
Signal
RCA Connector

RCA

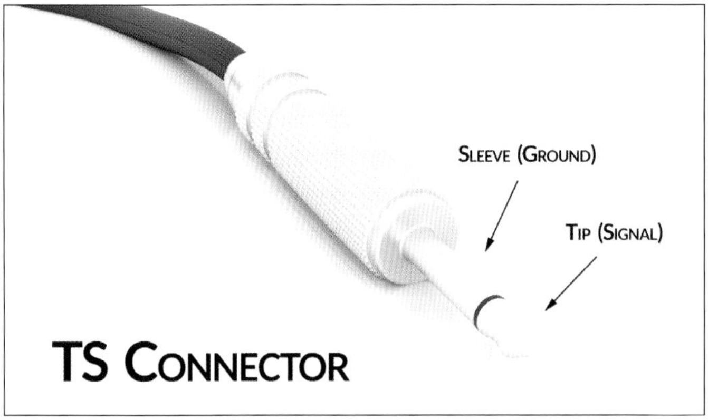
Sleeve (Ground)
Tip (Signal)
TS Connector

TS

120-pin ELCO connector can carry up to 40, balanced, analog audio signals

Elco

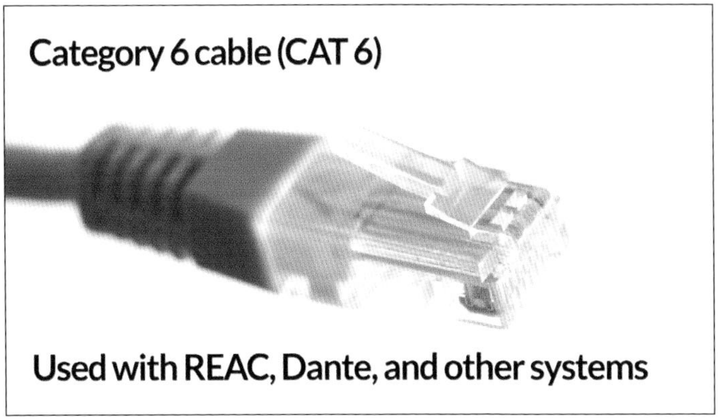

Cat-6

TOSLINK

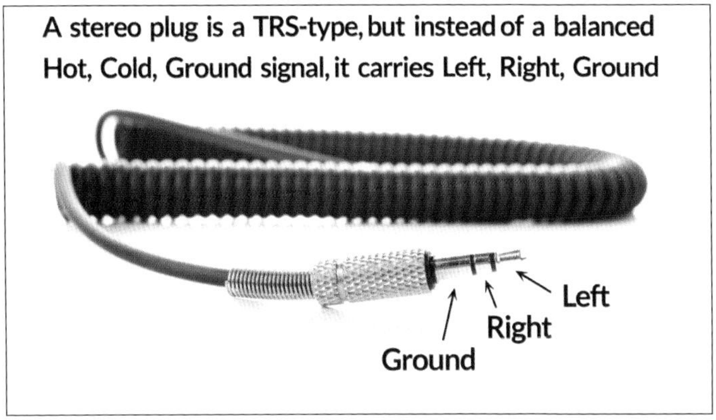

Mini Stereo ⅛"

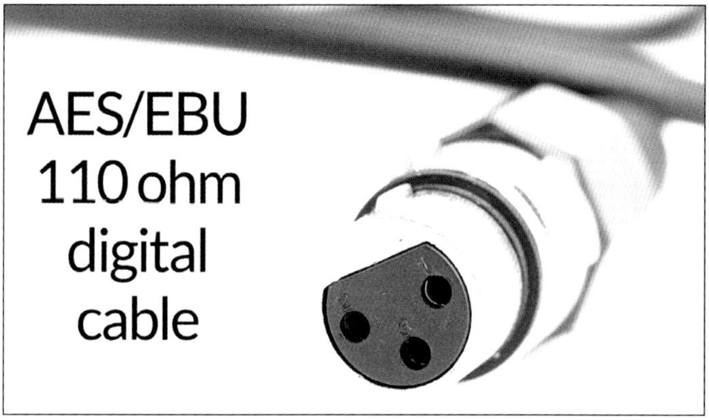

AES/EBU Digital

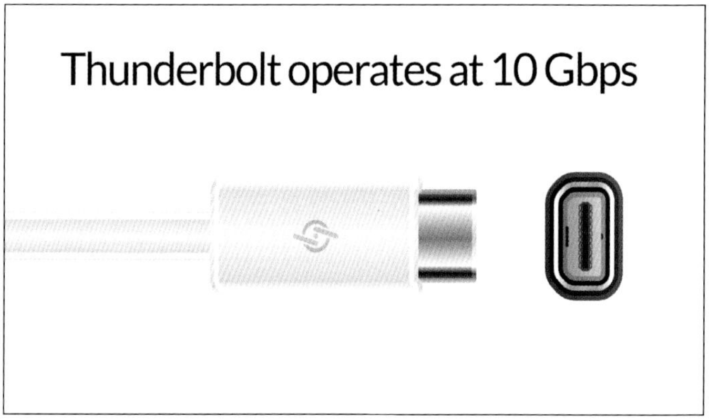

Thunderbolt

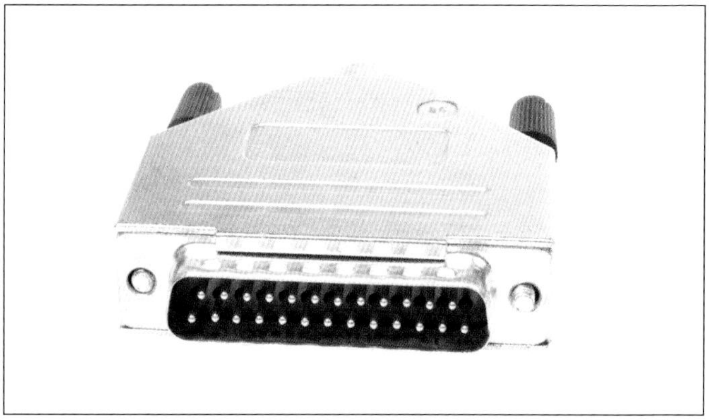

DB25

Speakon

BNC

Firewire 400

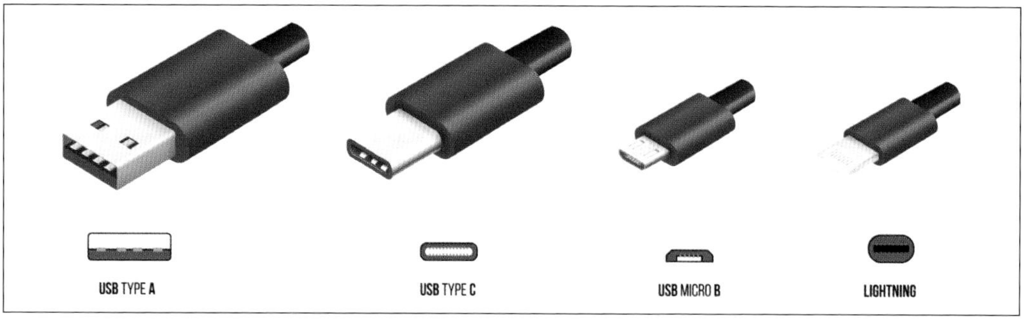

USB types

4

Speakers and Headphones

A speaker is a transducer. Like all transducers, a speaker changes one form of energy into another. It takes an electrical signal and converts it into acoustical energy that we can hear. In the studio, speakers, headphones, and in-ear monitors called IEMs are monitoring tools used by an engineer to make decisions on mic placement, EQ, compression, and balancing tracks in a mix. The quality of your monitors directly affects the quality of the music. If the music is not being reproduced with accuracy, the engineer's decisions will suffer, and the listener will not experience the music with the same power, dynamics, and emotion.

THE TRUTH

The truth is, transducers don't always tell the truth. Speaker and headphone components, amplification, internal electronics, cabling, power, noise, and especially the room you're in can all color the listening experience. Different sources sound different.

For example, car speakers, earbuds, and other consumer systems may have more or less low and high-frequency content than found in professional systems, but that doesn't mean you shouldn't use them as a cross reference during production. The bottom line is that it's okay that transducers aren't perfect, as long as you know their limitations and can still make musically sound decisions.

Arriving at the truth when monitoring is accomplished by having more than one reference. Variety builds trust. By listening to your tracks on different speakers, headphones, IEMs from a smartphone, and even on different systems in different rooms, you can learn to trust your ears and make great sounding recordings.

TYPES OF SPEAKERS

Speakers come in various types. For instance, a two-way monitor consists of a woofer and tweeter. An internal electronic crossover determines the point at which low and high frequencies are distributed to these components. A three-way speaker consists of a woofer, mid-range driver, and a tweeter. On this type of monitor, two electronic crossovers determine the point at which low, mid, and high frequencies are distributed to each of the three components.

A subwoofer, also called a *sub*, is an optional add-on monitor, which consists of one or more speakers that carry only low frequency signals. When a sub is used with a two- or three-way system, an integral, or separate bass manager, determines the crossover point that only allows low frequencies to pass to the sub.

Two- and three-way systems and subwoofers come in all sizes and prices. The good news is that modern speaker technology and manufacturing techniques have brought great-sounding products to affordable levels. Now, more than ever, there are excellent speakers in all price ranges.

SPEAKER COMPONENTS

Speaker components, called *drivers*, fall into two basic categories: woofers and tweeters. In a two-way system, the woofer handles low- and mid-frequency information, while a tweeter handles high frequencies. Woofers come in various sizes and can be made of everything from paper to more complex materials. A woofer's lightness and rigidity are factors that affect the sound. Tweeters can be made of silk or chemical elements like titanium and beryllium, which are used because of their unique properties. Heat dispersion and how well a material retains its shape are factors considered when manufacturing high-frequency speaker components.

Another method of speaker manufacturing uses a folded membrane, called a ribbon, for tweeters and mid-range components. This very thin and light diaphragm is folded in a way that allows air to be pushed out and pulled in during playback. The element's ability to move air in this way creates sound waves in the mid- or high-frequency ranges. The membrane starts out flat, and is hand folded using a special jig that allows for precise pleats to be created. The folded ribbon is glued for stability, then attached to the driver and metal housing used to mount the driver in the speaker cabinet. Wires are attached to the back of the driver, then each unit is tested to be sure the drivers offer a consistent listening experience. The ribbon driver, woofer, amplifier, and other components are then mounted in the speaker cabinet, which is tested again using a microphone, and test and measurement software. The finished speaker is then ready to ship to users worldwide.

What you see when you look at the front of a woofer is the cone and dust cover. The cone moves to create sound waves, while the dust cover simply keeps the internal part of the voice coil free of debris. The *surround* and *spider* is glued to the outer and inner edge of the cone and voice coil, then to the basket.

The *basket* is the skeletal structure of the woofer that holds all the components in place. Both the surround and spider work together to hold the speaker in place while it moves. At the back of the woofer is the voice coil, which consists of a *former* wrapped in wire that floats freely inside a large magnet. The voice coil works to push and pull the speaker in response to an amplified speaker level signal wired at the terminals.

The terminals at the back of the woofer, on the basket, are where the speaker level signal enters the woofer and causes the magnet and voice coil to move the cone. A tweeter is much smaller than a woofer because it carries only high-frequency content, which doesn't call for a large driver. It consists of a membrane, suspension, voice coil, and magnet, all held in place by a metal housing that is mounted in the speaker cabinet.

SPEAKER INPUTS AND FEATURES

Studio monitors are either active or passive. Active speakers come with an integral amplifier, while passive speakers need an external power amp. Most active consumer monitors have unbalanced RCA inputs, but active professional studio monitors may offer balanced and unbalanced analog inputs on RCA, XLR, and TRS connectors.

Some monitors also feature digital inputs that can take a signal directly from your digital audio workstation's A/D converter without leaving the digital domain. Other features vary and may include EQ, volume control, and boundary controls that adjust for proximity to desktops and walls. In some cases, a speaker may offer room correction, which is the ability to custom calibrate your speaker to your room using test tones, a microphone, and software.

HEADPHONES AND IN-EAR MONITORS

Headphones and in-ear monitors are valuable tools for monitoring while tracking, mixing, or doing overdubs. Headphones are one size fits all, and come in closed- or open-back designs. When mixing, either style will work. Open-back headphones offer an experience closer to listening to a speaker, while closed-back headphones and IEMs are better for recording, because they keep the mix isolated and out of the microphones.

Hearing signals from adjacent microphones placed on the same instrument or from headphones into a vocal mic is called leakage. While leakage between microphones may be desirable in a recording where two or more mics are set up in a single room, headphone leakage is considered bad and should be avoided at all costs. Headphone plugs are either quarter-inch TRS, or mini eighth-inch TRS. Although these look similar to the balanced plugs and cables we have learned about in past chapters, headphone plugs are unbalanced, with the ring and tip carrying the left and right signals. The sleeve at the base of the connector is the ground.

In-ear monitors, called IEMs, are commonly used in live sound, but are gaining popularity in recording studios because of their ability to isolate the mix when tracking, and they offer the engineer a custom listening experience while mixing. Because each IEM is custom built to fit only your ear, an impression must be made. The latest technology uses a digital, handheld device to create a 3D scan of the ear canal. The next step is to refine the scan using software, where imperfections are rounded and the ideal earpiece is shaped. The final product, which fits perfectly in your ear, is 3D printed and then attached to the drivers. IEM drivers, much like a speaker, are tuned to provide a balanced listening experience in the audible range.

MONITOR CONTROL

A monitor controller is a separate piece of gear where you, the engineer, design your listening experience. Some digital audio interfaces include monitor control, or it can be purchased as a standalone unit. Common features include volume control, the ability to switch between different pairs of speakers, mute, and volume output reduction via dim switches. Some monitor controllers offer room correction and remote control in addition to the basic controls mentioned above. Many controllers offer speaker outputs, plus separate headphone outputs with their own volume controls. These can be used for overdubs if you are recording live tracks in the same room as your speakers, and for supplying audio to musicians playing acoustic instruments.

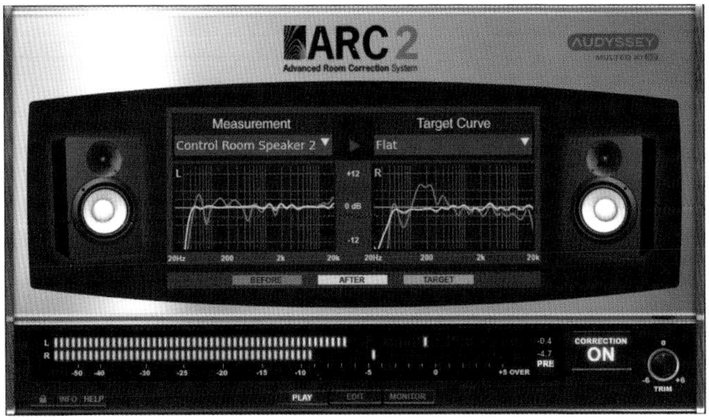

IK Multimedia's ARC System 2.5 features the MEMS measurement microphone, measurement software, and a correction plug-in for room correction

SPEAKERS AND HEADPHONES RECAP

Speakers come in two-way and three-way designs. A subwoofer, or *sub* is an optional add-on monitor that consists of one or more speakers carrying only low-frequency signals. Studio monitors are either active or passive. Active speakers come with an integral amplifier, while passive speakers need an external power amp. In-ear monitors, called IEMs, are commonly used in live sound, but are gaining popularity in recording studios because of their ability to isolate the mix when tracking, and they offer a custom listening experience while mixing. Open-back headphones can be better for mixing, giving you more of the experience of listening to speakers, while closed-back headphones and IEMs are better for recording, because they keep the mix isolated and out of the microphones.

5

DAWs and Converters

As we learned in the first chapter of the book, "Understanding Recording Signal Flow," the digital audio workstation, or DAW, sits squarely in the middle of the audio production and recording process. There are many types of DAWs that span a range of prices, from free to more expensive professional-grade systems that use third-party hardware interfaces for use with computers and laptops. The versatile digital audio workstation can take the place of many of the analog tools that once populated a recording studio, and at a fraction of the cost.

WHAT CAN A DAW DO?

At it's most basic level, the digital audio workstation mimics the basic building blocks found in a traditional analog recording studio, so it's easy to draw parallels between the old and new. For instance, the DAW is a recorder that's operational interface is much like the analog multitrack recorders used before the turn of the century. Like its predecessors, it uses individual tracks to record separate elements of a drum kit, or simultaneously record vocals, keyboards, guitars, amps, and other instruments.

A DAW is also a mixer, closely resembling an analog console. On both a console and DAW you'll find faders for adjusting the volume of individual tracks, panners for placing each element in the stereo field, auxiliary sends used for parallel, time-based effects such as reverb and delay, EQ for boosting or cutting various frequency bands, processors for manipulating the dynamic range of a track, buses for grouping tracks to a common channel, and meters for visual feedback showing the gain of the signal recorded on each track.

Editing is where the DAW has improved on techniques used in the past. Because you can see as well as hear the recorded waveforms, you can mouse around different parts of a waveform and perform many functions never possible with analog tape-based editing.

But where the DAW clearly steps into the future is in its ability to expand or contract depending on the needs of the session. This is called a *virtual environment.* For example, when you first open a DAW session, there are no tracks or mix channels, but you can quickly add as many tracks and mix channels as you need, up to the limits of the hardware and software. You can also call up powerful processors called plug-ins that allow you to manipulate audio in many creative ways.

WHAT IS A PLUG-IN?

A plug-in is a companion piece of software available on individual or grouped channels within a DAW session. Many DAWs come with their own plug-ins, or you can buy compatible plug-ins from third party developers—there are hundreds to choose from.

In a session, each plug-in instance uses DSP, or digital signal processing, to achieve its outcome. DSP is provided by the computer's own processing power, or from an external card or interface that supplies the computer power necessary to run the plug-in. DSP is a finite resource, so you may run out of available power to run plug-ins in a session. There are steps you can take to optimize and reuse DSP that we will explore later in the book.

Plug-ins are versatile. They can emulate instruments such as guitars, drums, strings, pianos, and more. They also mimic popular EQs, time-based effects, and compressors from the past, as well as new types of processors allowing the operator to perform new kinds of audio manipulation. For instance, software like Synchro Arts Revoice Pro is able to musically tune vocals. Music and film sound professionals also use Revoice Pro to align vocals or voiceovers. In a song, this means you can tighten up vocal harmonies, creating a believable and musical synchronization between parts.

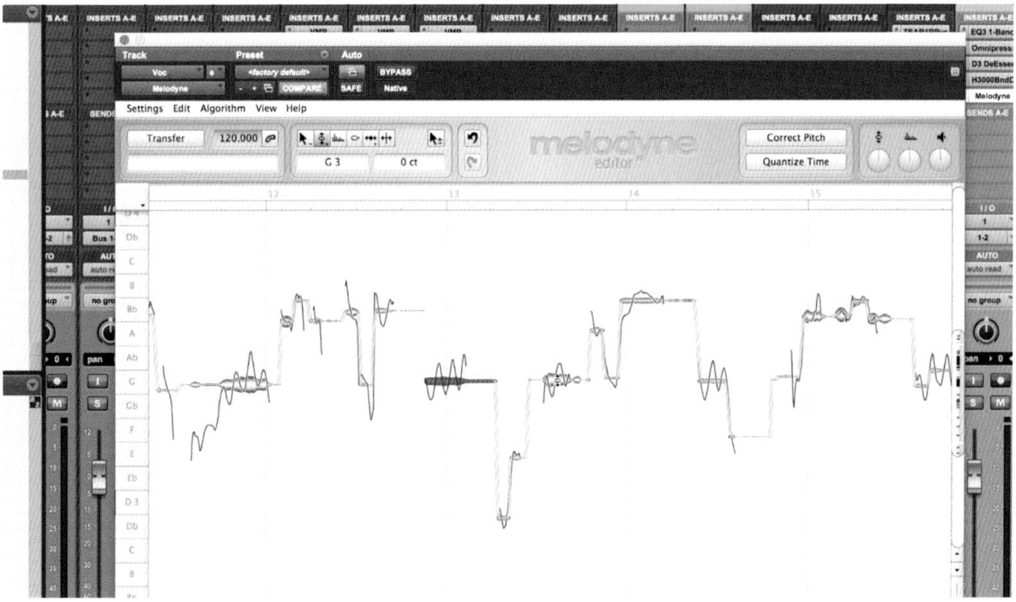

Other tuning software, such as Celemony's Melodyne, Synchro Arts Revoice Pro, and Antares Auto-Tune, works on similar principles and has redefined vocal processing in popular music, creating signature vocal sounds used by many popular artists.

Plug-ins can easily be called up by choosing them from a list on a channel's insert. An insert is a point in a channel's signal flow where the signal may be detoured through a plug-in. This is called a serial connection because 100% of the signal is sent through the plug-in. You can also use the DAW's auxiliary sends on the channels to set up plug-ins in parallel, so many channels can be sent through a plug-in. A parallel connection allows you to use a plug-in across one or more audio tracks and saves DSP because more than one channel is accessing a single plug-in. The advantage of using plug-ins is that they are less expensive than their hardware counterparts. A single plug-in may be used on many channels, whereas a hardware processor can only be used on a single channel.

DIGITAL AUDIO CONVERSION

Digital sound and pictures are everywhere—from the latest movies on the big screen, to television streamed from a satellite or cable, to music, text, photos, and video on our handheld smart devices. Even the sound at live concerts is mixed on a digital console and recorded to a DAW using many of the plug-ins found in a recording studio. It's all ones and zeroes.

But before a sound or image can be recorded, processed, edited, and mixed in software, it must first be converted to a digital format. Then, once it leaves the software, it must be converted back to an analog signal to be played or viewed again. This is the job of the A/D and D/A converter.

In order to understand how sound is converted, let's compare it to a digital image. The basic building block of a digital image is a pixel. The more pixels there are in an image, the better the quality. A high definition image is considered to be the best that technology can offer, and HD standards are changing all the time. The same is true for audio.

The first analog recording of a human voice, made on a phonautograph, is over 150 years old and was recorded seventeen years before Edison invented the phonograph. The quality is bad, but over time higher definition recording formats took shape. The first commercial digital recording was made by Denon in 1971, and twelve years later in 1982, the CD became a widely-accepted, digital-commercial format operating at 44.1 kHz and 16-bits.

But what do the numbers mean? In digital audio, the key terms to remember are sample rate and bit depth. The sample rate is measured in kilohertz and denotes the number of samples taken in a second. For example, a sound wave captured at 44.1 kHz represents 44,100 samples per second. The bit depth represents each sample's volume, or amplitude, and is also called dynamic range.

Like a pixel is to an image, a sample is to sound—the more you have, the better the recording. It all boils down to simple math. The maximum frequency recorded cannot be higher than half the sample rate.

So what's the best sample and bit rate? Digital recording can be better understood once you know the limits of our ears. The frequency range of human hearing is 20 Hz to 20 kHz. So to cover the range of human hearing, you need to double the sample rate. The CD rate of 44.1 kHz mentioned earlier covers that and more, but is it the best? Does audio quality increase if you sample beyond the range of human hearing? That's where there is some controversy, and let's just say there will never be agreement. The upside of recording at higher sample rates is an undeniable increase in quality, while the downside is a lower DAW track count, reduced plug-in availability, and much larger files. As an engineer, once you assess the needs of your project, the choice of sample and bit rate on each session is up to you. Just remember, you're recording music and making art. Enjoy yourself!

6

Mic Choices and Placement

In the first chapter of the book, "Understanding Recording Signal Flow," we learned that studio microphones fall into two basic categories: dynamic and condenser. But the truth is, within each category there are hundreds of mics to choose from. So how do you pick the right one for the job? Asking the right questions about your microphones before the talent arrives is what separates a great recording from a good one. For example, when is it better to use a dynamic mic rather than a condenser? How is a tube mic different from a solid-state mic? When is it safe to use a ribbon mic, and are all ribbon mics the same? How do you place each mic, and what is the best polar pattern for each application? You'll learn the answers to these questions and more as we progress through this chapter.

Whether you have access to a vast collection of microphones or even just a few, knowing the general characteristics and features of the various models, and then using that information to pick the right mics for your session will result in better sounding tracks.

MICROPHONE FEATURES

Many microphones share common features. For instance, they are either front address, meaning the capsule points out of the front end of the mic, or side address, where the capsule points out the side of the mic. Mics that address from the front or side may look alike, but may not work as you'd think. For example, both of these mics look similar: they both have grills on either side of a solid bar across the top, but the left mic is side address, and the right mic is front address. The only way to know the difference for sure is study and experience.

A front or side address microphone placed properly is said to be "on-axis" to the source, meaning the diaphragm or ribbon is pointing towards the source. A microphone's "off-axis" point is the side, top, or back—and depending on the polar pattern, can be used to reject unwanted sound. In this case, the tom mics are rejecting the cymbals.

It's also common for microphones to require phantom power. This power is supplied by the microphone preamp and is sent along the mic cable to the microphone. It's important to know which types of mics need phantom power because there exists the risk of damage. For example, condenser and active ribbon mics need phantom power, but it should never be applied to a passive ribbon mic. A tube microphone has its own power supply and never needs phantom power. How do you know which is which? Study and experience are the only way to know for sure, and if you're not sure, always ask before you push the phantom power button.

Phantom Power Guide

Passive Ribbon	Dynamic Moving Coil	Active Ribbon	Condenser	Tube Condenser
DANGER! Never Apply Phantom Power	No Phantom Needed	Phantom Power Needed	Phantom Power Needed	No Phantom Needed Tube mics have their own power supply

the blackbird academy
FOUNDATION SERIES

FREQUENCY RESPONSE

In a perfect world, all microphones would capture all frequencies equally, but this is far from the case. As you can see from these frequency response charts, every microphone's frequency response is different. And even if the responses are close, they can still sound different. The lesson here is to use a frequency response chart for general information, but never as a tool to make a sonic value judgment. Ultimately, your ears are the best way to judge a microphone.

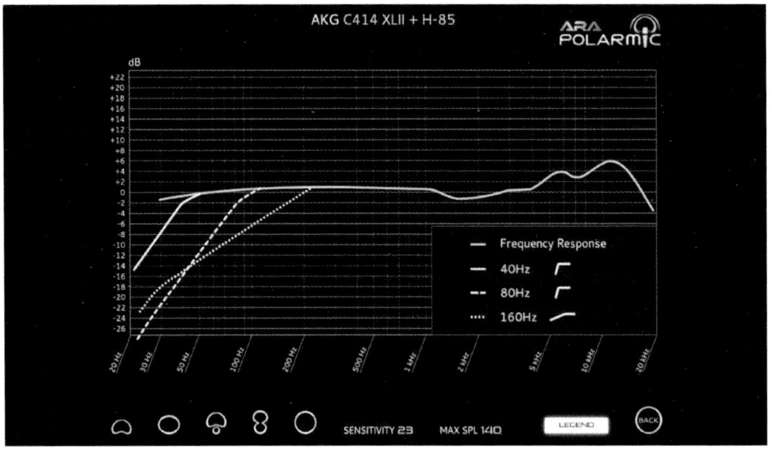
AKG C414 XLII + H-85
ARA POLARMIC
dB
Frequency Response
40Hz
80Hz
160Hz
SENSITIVITY 23
MAX SPL 140
LEGEND
BACK

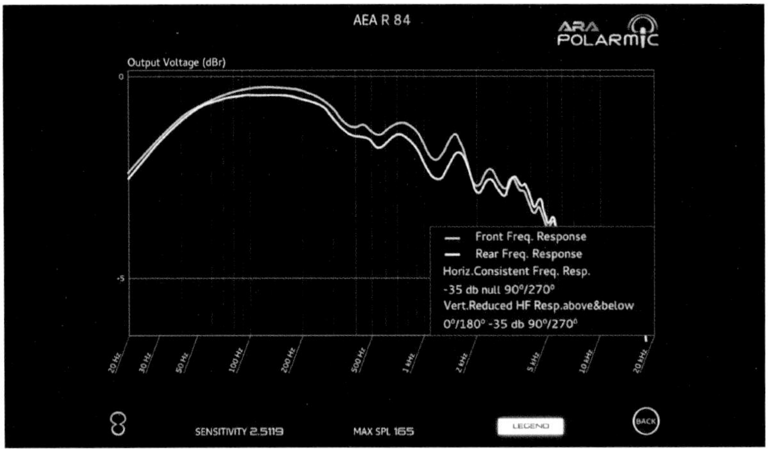
AEA R 84
ARA POLARMIC
Output Voltage (dBr)
Front Freq. Response
Rear Freq. Response
Horiz.Consistent Freq. Resp.
-35 db null 90°/270°
Vert.Reduced HF Resp.above&below
0°/180° -35 db 90°/270°
SENSITIVITY 2.5119
MAX SPL 165
LEGEND
BACK

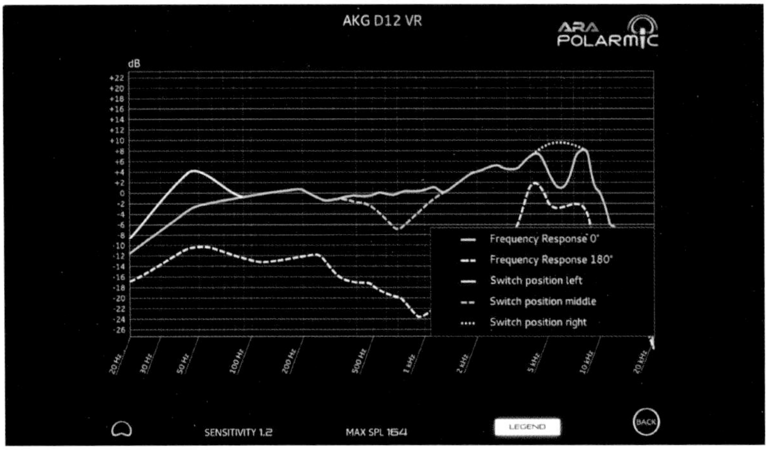
AKG D12 VR
ARA POLARMIC
dB
Frequency Response 0°
Frequency Response 180°
Switch position left
Switch position middle
Switch position right
SENSITIVITY 1.2
MAX SPL 164
LEGEND
BACK

DIRECTIONALITY AND POLAR PATTERNS

All microphones have a directionality, also known as a polar pattern. This is how a microphone "hears" sound from every angle both on- and off-axis. The most common patterns are cardioid, figure 8, and omni. Each has its personality and uses in the studio.

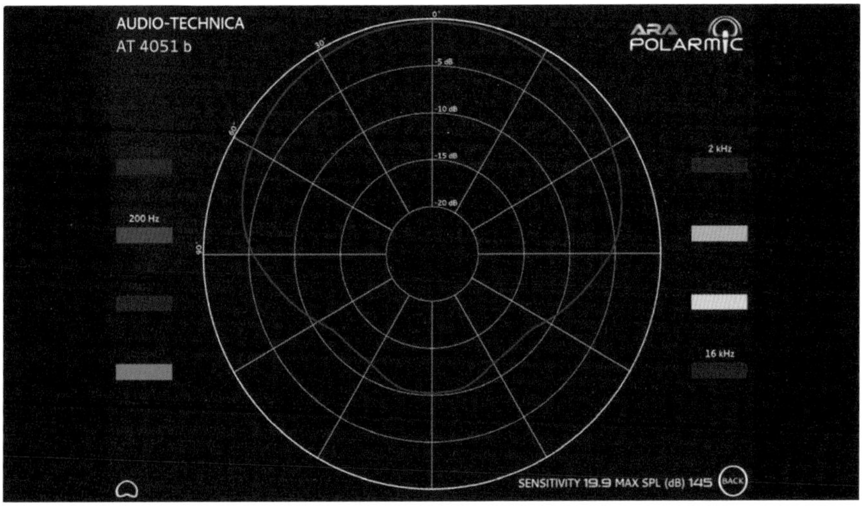

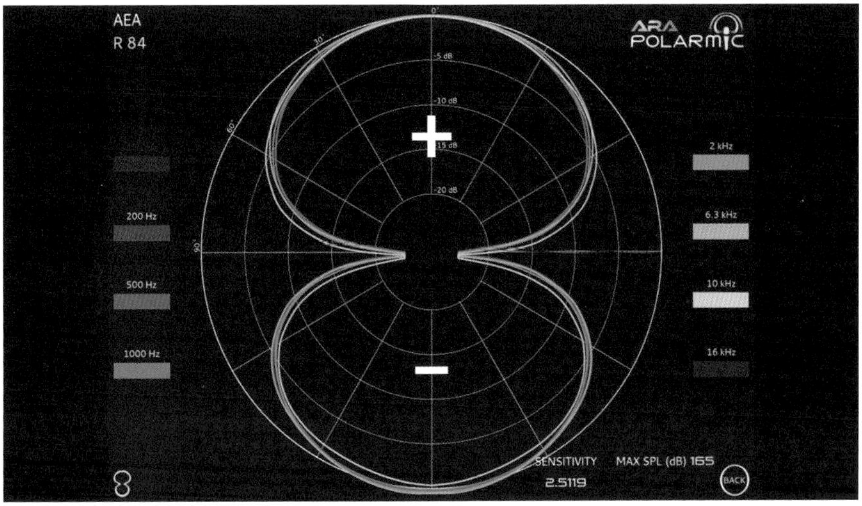

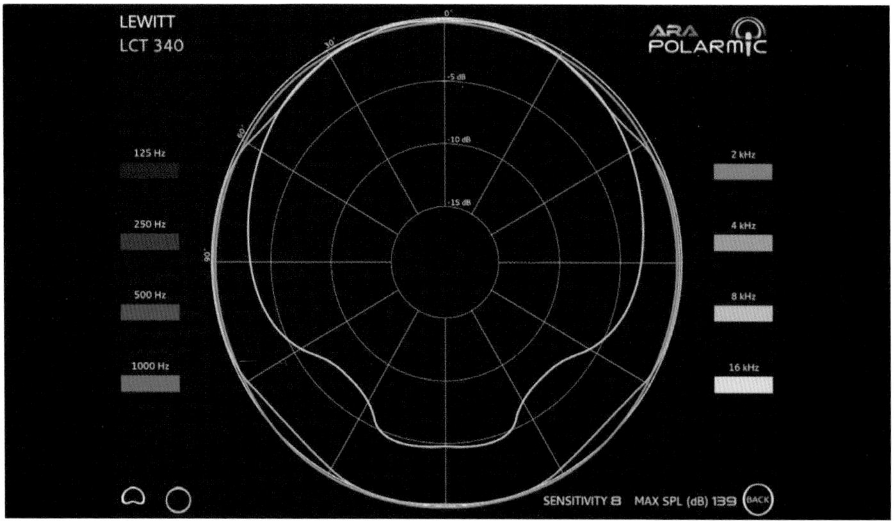

The cardioid pattern is most sensitive on-axis and becomes less and less sensitive as you move to 180 degrees off-axis. Think of this pattern as like aiming a flashlight—the microphone hears best wherever it's pointed, or where you would see the most light. You would use a cardioid pattern when you want to reject other instruments close by. For instance, this cardioid hi-hat mic is turned off-axis to reject the cymbals and snare, while the snare and tom mics are off-axis to the cymbals.

Here you can see the use of four cardioid microphones placed on-axis to each singer and guitar. This placement acts to isolate each performer by rejecting audio at the off-axis point and minimizing leakage.

The figure 8 pattern looks just like the number 8, and is focused more or less equally at the front and back of the microphone. It's important to note that the front of this pattern is in positive polarity, and the back in negative polarity. Most ribbon microphones are figure 8 by nature, but there are exceptions such as cardioid ribbons.

The figure 8 pattern is much less directional than cardioid, and is open to all kinds of creative applications for recording drums, room miking, guitar and bass cabinets, horns, and other acoustic instruments.

The omni pattern is best described as a beach ball with a microphone in the middle. The mic "hears" in a 360 degree pattern—front, back, top, bottom, and sides. While this is how omni works in theory, the truth is that an omni mic is not omni at all frequencies. As you can see in this comparison of omni polar patterns on different microphones, higher frequencies are more directional than lower frequencies, whereas lower frequencies are more circular.

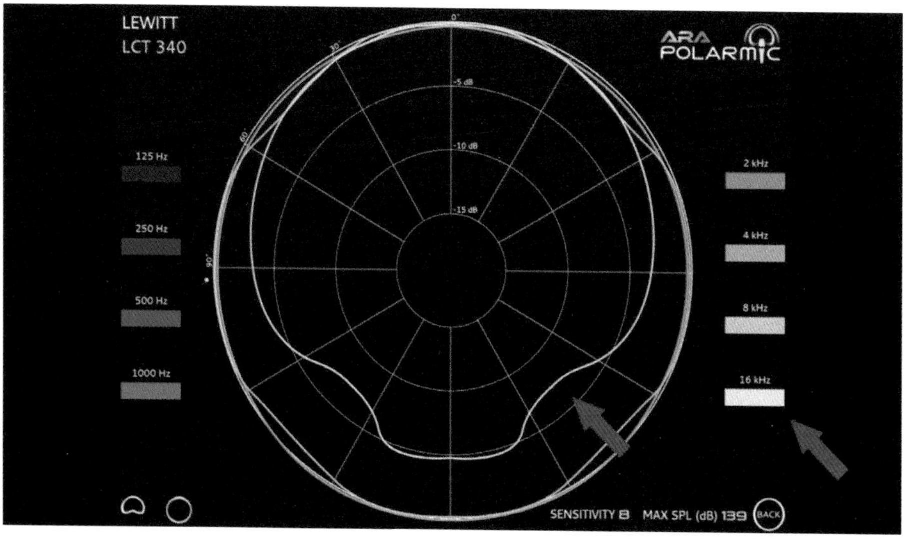

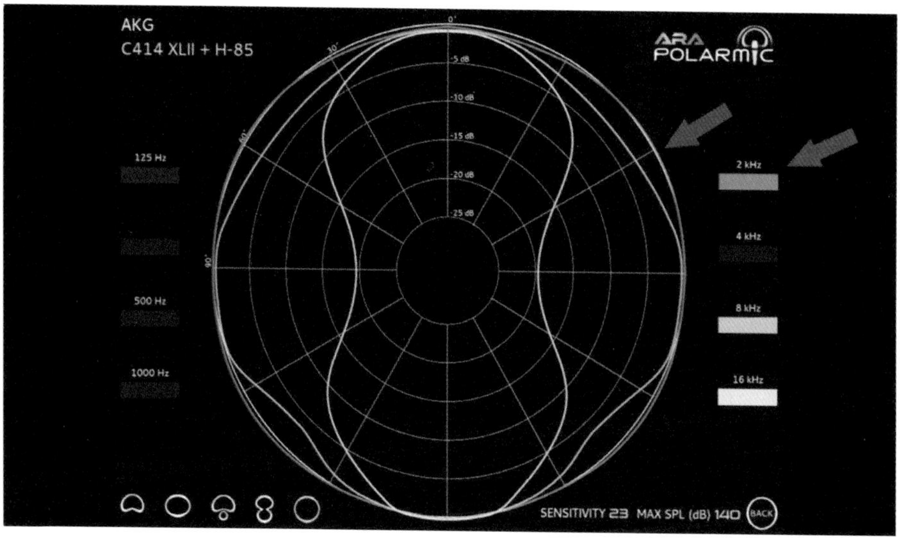

Because of its unique qualities, the omni pattern excels in situations where accuracy off-axis is important (such as in classical recording), when used as room mics, and with specialized microphone arrangements, such as the decca tree shown here.

PROXIMITY EFFECT AND MORE

Another consideration when choosing and placing microphones is the proximity effect, which is an increase of low frequencies as the microphone gets closer to the source. This is not necessarily a bad thing and may be desired when recording upright bass, drums, piano, and other instruments. As an engineer, you can play with the amount of proximity by simply moving the mic closer or farther away from the source.

As an engineer, it's important to know that even if microphones have the same polar pattern and frequency response, they may still sound different. As you can see in these polar diagrams from the Arapolarmic app, the patterns change slightly, depending on the frequency, and also change from model to model. The truth is that all mics don't sound the same, and this is great news. The varieties of microphones add to the sonic palette engineers use to record memorable music.

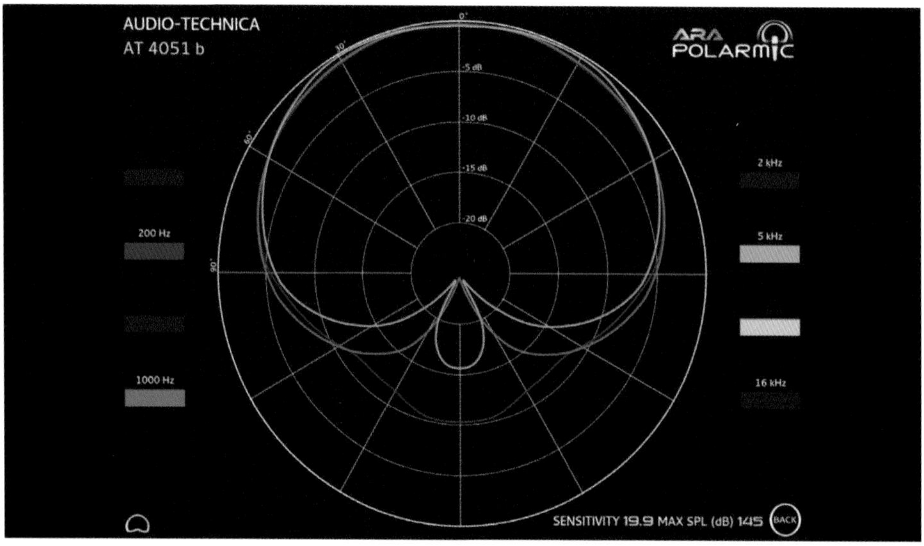

VOICING, ROLL-OFF, AND PAD

Just as some microphones allow you to switch polar patterns, there are mics that allow you to change frequency sensitivities. This is called *voicing*. On the Lauten Eden and Atlantis mics, you can switch between forward, neutral, and gentle voicings. You can do the same on the AKG D12VR microphone, which is optimized for kick drum. For example, you may want to voice your mic to be more sensitive at low frequencies when recording kick drums and toms, but more sensitive to higher frequencies when miking cymbals or percussion.

Other features on microphones vary and may include a roll-off and pad. A roll-off switch engages a high-pass filter.

A pad reduces the amount of gain at the output of the microphone, so you don't overload the preamp. A pad is commonly used when the signal is especially loud, like a drum kit, guitar cabinet, or other high SPL source. SPL stands for *sound pressure level*, and describes the loudness of a source measured in decibels. For example, average conversational speech is about 60dB SPL, whereas a jet engine is very loud at 130dB SPL.

MONO AND STEREO PLACEMENT

Mono recording is accomplished with a single microphone close to the source. The type used and distance from the source depends greatly on what you're recording, the sound pressure level, and the desired outcome in the mix. One example for close recording of toms and snare is to place the microphone four fingers off the rim, then point it at the center of the drum.

When placing a microphone on a guitar or bass cabinet, center the microphone where the dust cover meets the cone near the center of the speaker. To record a wider array of frequencies and add more personality in the mix, it's a good idea to use two types of microphones, such as the Shure SM57 and Royer R-121 pictured here.

When recording vocals, be sure to isolate the singer from the band, and use a cardioid or figure 8 microphone. The cardioid pattern brings more intimacy to the voice in the mix, and a figure 8 microphone can also be used to isolate an instrument at the same time. For instance, in this application, you see a Shure SM7 used with a round pop filter in front to protect the capsule from any puffs of air, called plosives.

In this photo, a vocalist plays an acoustic guitar miked with a Beyerdynamic M160, which features a hypercardioid pattern that quickly becomes less sensitive off-axis.

Using two directional microphones better separates the voice from the guitar, and the guitar from the vocal track, making it easier to balance these elements in a mix.

When miking instruments like acoustic guitar, upright bass, dobro, and other stringed instruments, one or two microphones can be spaced in front of the instrument, then panned in stereo or mono, depending on the instrument and mix. When placing two microphones as a stereo pair, it's important to follow some basic, time-tested techniques often used by professional engineers.

For example, the XY technique, also called a coincident pair, places two cardioid capsules stacked on top of each other and aimed at 90 degrees. This technique can cover a wide range of applications, from drum overheads, miking of small ensembles like string quartets, room mics, and more. When you use this XY technique with ribbon mics, it's called the blumlein technique, named after Alan Blumlein, an early adopter and inventor of stereo recording techniques.

NOS is a stereo miking technique named for the Dutch Broadcast Foundation. Like the XY technique, two cardioid microphones are placed at 90 degrees, but the capsules are spaced 30 centimeters, or just under 12 inches, apart. NOS would be used when a larger recording angle is desired.

Another similar technique, developed by the French called ORTF, uses two cardioid microphones placed at 110 degrees and 17 centimeters, or about 6 and ½ inches, apart. Because of the width of the angle in this technique, the microphones can be placed farther from the source, and still provide a believable stereo image. For the best results with XY, NOS, and ORTF, the microphones should be cardioid pairs from the same manufacturer.

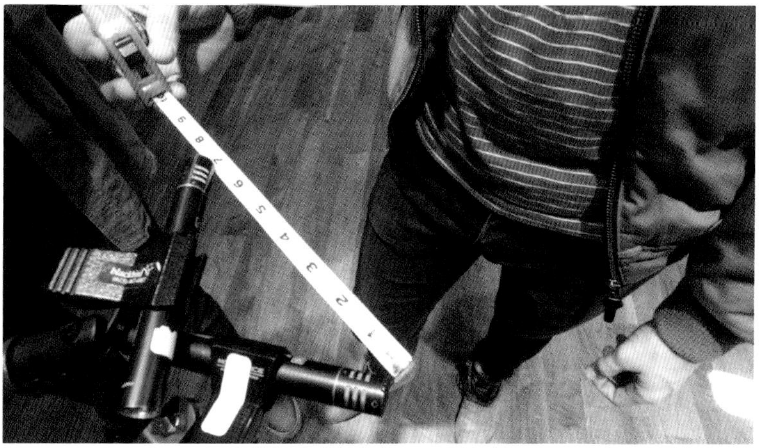

Other techniques place the microphones farther apart and follow a simple 3-to-1 ratio to maintain proper phase between the mics. The 3-to-1 rule states that for every unit of distance from the source, the microphones should be at least 3 units apart. As you can see in this example, the microphones placed closely over the piano strings follow this rule.

Another technique for spacing a pair over a drum kit uses two cardioid or figure 8 microphones of the same model spaced equally apart from the snare drum. This keeps the center-panned snare drum in phase across the stereo pair of overheads, and also accurately renders the toms and cymbals left to right.

Another stereo technique, called a decca tree, widely spaces three microphones. It was refined by the engineering team at Decca Records in the middle of the last century, and is still commonly used for orchestral recording. Although the measurements and microphones may vary, the basic technique uses three omni microphones of the same model spaced evenly left, right, and forward of a center point. You can use easily obtained tools like tape measures and laser levels to measure the distances and accurately place the mics using common studio mic stands. Or, you can purchase a foldable, commercially available microphone array from a pro audio dealer.

BOUNDARY MICS AND OTHERS

Some out-of-the-ordinary microphones used in studio recording include the LoFrEQ from Solomon Mics. It's a speaker reverse-wired into the role of a microphone. While not a new concept, this compact and affordable microphone specializes in capturing low frequencies around a drum kit or bass amp.

Another specialty transducer you'll find in the studio is a boundary mic, which was first used for install recording and sound reinforcement in theater and boardroom applications because of its low profile. However, this doesn't keep audio engineers from using it successfully in studio applications. One type of popular boundary mic is the Shure Beta 91, a phantom-powered half-cardioid microphone often used for kick-drum recording.

The MB OSS-II is a stereo boundary microphone incorporating two omnidirectional microphones mounted on a plate. In between them is a sound-absorbing barrier called a jecklin disk. The concept was pioneered by Swiss recording engineer Jurg Jecklin and is called the optimum stereo signal recording technique. Like all boundary mics, they can be attached to a wall or placed on the floor, inside the lid of a piano, on studio glass, or any on other flat surface.

MIC CHOICES AND PLACEMENT RECAP

- Microphones are either front or side address, and have on- and off-axis points.
- It's important to know when to apply phantom power to avoid damaging some types of microphones.
- No two microphones sound the same. It's best to learn to trust your ears rather than rely on documentation when choosing the correct type and model.
- A microphone's polar pattern describes how it hears sound from any direction. Some patterns will give you more isolation from surrounding instruments than others.
- The proximity effect is a characteristic shared by all directional microphones, where low frequency increases when a microphone is placed closer to the source.
- Voicing, roll-off, and pad are three features found on some microphones. They allow you to tailor the mic's frequency characteristics, compensate for the proximity effect, and lower the output of the microphone to avoid overloading the preamp stage.
- Stereo miking techniques include XY, NOS, ORTF, spaced pair, and a decca tree. Each of these techniques requires precise measurement and setup to assure phase coherence between the transducers.

7

Managing Gain and Distortion

As consumers, we deal with sound all the time. Whether you're home or on the go, it's an easy thing to push the up or down button on a TV remote, adjust the volume when listening to music from a tablet or smartphone, or turn up the sound on your car radio. It's all usually a one-step process. But as an engineer producing music for these devices, you will encounter many more ways to adjust gain along the recording and mixing signal path.

These can include volume pots on guitars, basses, DI boxes, and preamps for adjusting source gain; hardware and software time-based effects, such as reverb and delay; line trims on consoles and plug-ins used to boost level at the top of a channel; plug-in and hardware compressors used to control dynamic range and EQ for sweetening tracks; plus all manner of faders along the signal path before, inside, and after the DAW—including sends and master faders. Finally, there are the volume controls for the headphones or speakers where you finally hear your work.

Before we learn the mechanics of setting volume along the signal path, it's important to know two important terms. A *gain stage* is a point in signal flow where volume can be increased or decreased. The goal is to set each stage so the signal maintains its quality from the source to the listener by preventing added distortion and noise.

The second term is *unity gain*, the setting of a gain stage so the signal level is neither raised nor lowered in level. In other words, the signal passing through a fader or pot is the same volume before and after the stage. Depending on the device, there may or may not be a determination where unity gain resides. On a fader, unity gain is marked by the number zero. On a pot, it can also be marked with the number zero or have a *detent*—a point where a rotary parks itself in position, usually at twelve o'clock. No matter how it's established, unity gain is the way to take multiple gain stages in your signal flow out of play so you can establish one, or possibly two, as the predominate way of boosting or cutting signal gain.

DEMYSTIFYING ZERO

As we learned in the second chapter of the book, "Electrical Levels in Audio Production," decibels can be confusing, so it's important to clarify how unity gain and analog and digital meters work. Unity gain is represented as 0 dB, and it may seem to make sense that zero means no sound at all, but this is not the case in pro audio. Instead, the term used to represent silence is *negative infinity*, and is symbolized by a sideways figure 8. You'll usually find this symbol at the bottom of a fader. At negative infinity, no sound will pass to the next stage. So if 0 dB is unity gain on an analog device, then what's the zero at the top of a digital meter? This is digital zero, or dB full scale, notated as dBFS—the maximum amount of gain before clipping and distortion.

Gain staging affects audio quality. Clipping your converters above 0 dBFS should be avoided. Now let's look at some techniques that will keep your tracks sounding great.

BEING THE MASTER OF YOUR SIGNAL CHAIN

Sometimes it's easy to determine the best way to manage gain along the signal path. For example, if you're recording a single mic using just a preamp with a single gain stage feeding the recorder, it's simple: the preamp is your only gain stage. As you turn up the preamp, look at your DAW's channel meter and adjust the gain so it isn't too low or too high. The optimal level is usually two-thirds to three-quarters up the meter, just enough to allow for occasional peaks. On an analog VU meter, the signal should peak at, or just below, 0 dB.

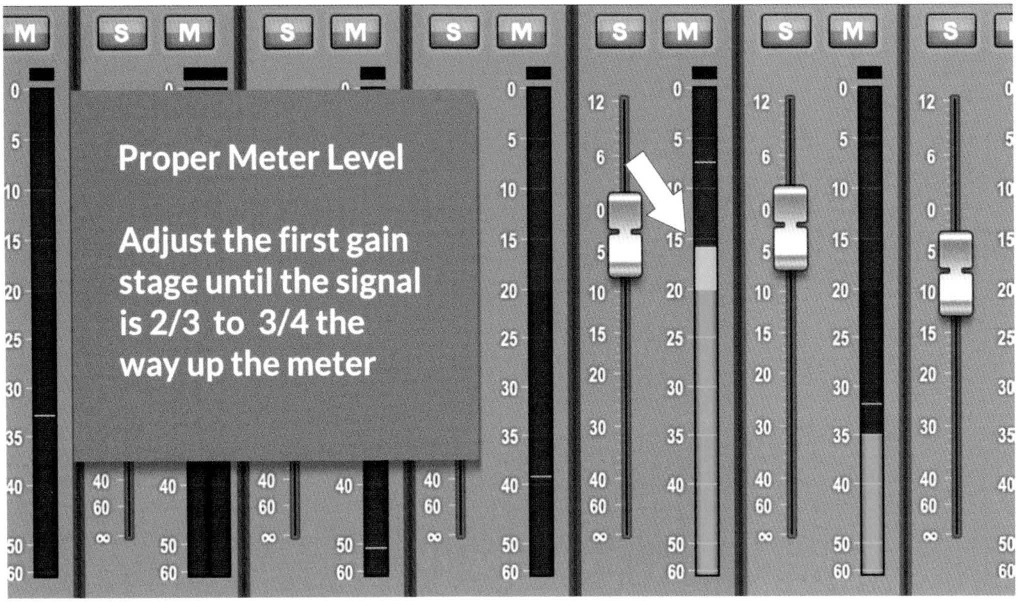

Setting levels can be different for different instruments. For example, if the track has spikey transients like a drum or a percussively-played bass or piano, then you'd leave more room at the top of the meter to accommodate the peaks.

One gain stage is easy, but what if your signal chain includes a preamp, a compressor with input and output gain, and a multi-band EQ? This is where setting gain becomes more complex. Let's start with the components.

As we learned in the first chapter of this book, "Understanding Recording Signal Flow," the preamp comes after the microphone or DI. Next comes processing on the way to the analog-to-digital converter. In this example, the preamp comes first and should be your main gain stage. But it's important to first neutralize the processors so you can get a base level from the preamp. Different models of compressors may have one or two gain stages marked "input" or "output." Start by setting these to unity gain, then raising the compressor's threshold to maximum. You can also use the bypass feature if available, which turns off the processor's functions. This will allow a signal to pass through the device at unity gain without being compressed.

Next, zero the EQ by setting the boost-and-cut control for each band to unity gain, or use the bypass function as mentioned before. It's important to understand that with these stages set to unity gain and processing not applied, it's almost as if they didn't exist—your preamp is still the master control for setting the level to your DAW. This is your starting point.

After your base level is set, apply compression and EQ while keeping an ear on the outcome and an eye on your DAW and processor's meters. Using these methods will maintain the quality of the tracks in your session.

You just read a dizzying number of terms and tips for adjusting level along the signal path, but don't panic! Ultimately, it's all about the music. By following some simple rules, you can be well on your way to producing great-sounding tracks while maintaining the honesty, integrity, and feeling of a performance.

WHAT IS DISTORTION?

Distortion and noise are caused by changes in a signal as it travels through cables and gear along the signal path. It can be caused by gain settings, cables, gear, and electronics, or the RF and EMF we learned about in the third chapter of this book, "Cables and Connectors."

While there are many kinds of distortion, the type we deal with most often is harmonic distortion and is measured as THD. THD can be put into two categories: even- or odd-order. As a general rule, even-order distortion produced by tube microphones and other gear is more desirable than odd-order, but beauty is in the eye of the beholder.

For example, we've been talking about proper gain settings as a means of avoiding distortion and noise, but what if we *want* to add distortion to our recording? Many styles of music rely on distortion as an effect. Distortion adds edge to the bass track, making it sit higher in the mix.

True analog distortion can be provided by using a tube hardware device like a guitar amp, microphone, preamp, compressor, or EQ, before or after the recording. Transformers also add their own color, especially when driven hard. Plug-in simulations of guitar amps and pedals offer various styles and colors of distortion at a fraction of the price of an analog device. Opinions certainly differ on the best gear and methods for adding distortion, but whatever the approach, distortion can be beautiful.

MANAGING GAIN AND DISTORTION RECAP

- A *gain stage* is a point in a signal flow where volume can be increased or decreased.
- *Unity gain*, often represented by the number zero, is the setting of a gain stage, so the signal level is neither raised nor lowered.
- Zero at the top of a digital meter stands for dB full scale, which is notated as dBFS. It is the maximum amount of gain achievable before clipping and distortion occur.
- The optimal level when setting your record volume is usually two-thirds to three-quarters up the meter, just enough to allow for occasional peaks.
- THD, or total harmonic distortion, can be put into two categories: even- or odd-order. As a general rule, even-order distortion produced by tube microphones and other gear is more desirable than odd-order.
- When using a chain of gear that has many gain stages along the signal path, use your microphone preamp as the main gain stage, then add EQ and compression. As you apply processing, watch the meters at each device or the DAW and adjust the level appropriately to avoid clipping.

8

Analog and Digital Processing

Analog and digital processors are powerful tools used to alter the sound of your tracks when recording and mixing. These can be EQs and filters for adjusting tone, dynamic processors like compressors and limiters for managing gain, plus other processors for pitch-shifting, transient-shaping, applying reverb, delay, and more. There are three opportunities to add processing along the signal path—either before, after, or inside the DAW. It's important to know the differences because some choices may be permanent, while others may introduce unacceptable latency during recording.

Latency in digital recording is caused by two things: A/D and D/A conversion, and plug-ins. While encoder/decoder latency is a fixed number dependent on each specific converter and the sample rate, plug-in latency varies and depends on the process. For example, the three plug-ins you see here vary between 99, 1,113, and 37 samples of latency—quite a difference!

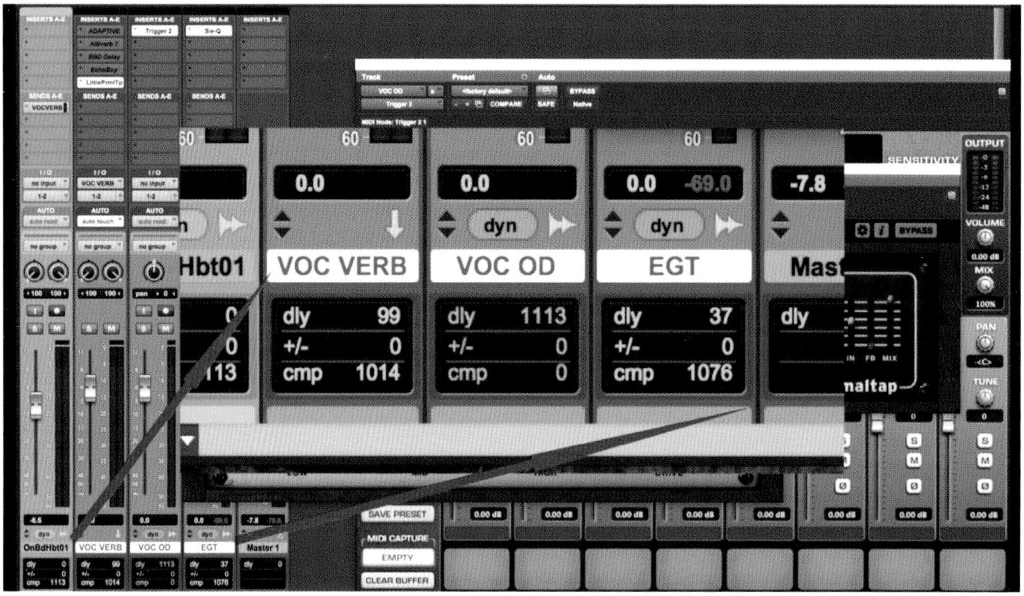

Latency is usually not a problem when you're the only listener. For example, when you're mixing, the DAW's delay compensation feature will take care of the delay caused by converters and plug-ins making it indiscernible.

Think of delay compensation as a traffic light that makes all tracks wait for the track with the longest delay, then allows them all to leave the system at the same time. But when recording when musicians are playing and listening back in real time, converter latency, plug-in processing, and delay compensation can be a groove killer.

Even with just a small amount of system latency, the delay between the performance and playback would sound unacceptable and be a distraction to the creative process. But by knowing the rules, it can be avoided.

OVERCOMING LATENCY

There are a few ways to reduce latency so it has minimal impact on the recording process. The first is to adjust the hardware buffer in your DAW. The buffer size sets the time allowed for the computer to do the math that gets your recording in and out of the box. The downside of a larger buffer is unacceptable latency as we discussed earlier. But when the buffer size is too small, it may cause system lag, computer crashing, and ticks and pops during playback. The best solution is to find the buffer setting that works best for your system and stick with that.

Another solution is to use an interface with low-latency monitoring. Many affordable audio interfaces offer this as a front-panel either/or feature. This gives you the ability to monitor either the input source before it hits the converters, or the DAW's output. This type of system is both an affordable and effective way to record overdubs in a home studio. But for larger setups where you need to record a higher number of inputs and outputs, many studios worldwide use professional systems like Pro Tools HD. Because of Pro Tools HD's proprietary cards and interfaces, latency can be lowered below a millisecond, essentially eliminating the converter and processing delay heard when using other native systems. Unlike Pro Tools HD, a native system relies 100% on the host computer's processing power.

So buffer size, direct monitoring, and professional systems are effective ways to deal with latency, but what about processing? Remember, plug-ins add latency too. One solution is to apply analog EQ or dynamics before the DAW, eliminating plug-ins from the signal path altogether. Analog processing is recorded with the signal, so it's permanent. It also exhibits zero latency because hard-wired analog signals travel near the speed of light—fast enough to circle the earth over seven times in one second. For this reason, analog hardware-processing applied before the DAW is a common studio practice when tracking a band, or while recording overdubs.

Another solution is to apply analog EQ or dynamics after the DAW. This type of processing is not recorded with the signal so it's temporary and non-destructive. Analog processing applied after the DAW is used when you don't want to commit to a sound while tracking or overdubbing, but would rather apply hardware or plug-in processing at a later time during the mix when latency isn't an issue.

The last, and most common types of processing found in modern production are applied inside the DAW using plug-ins. This type of processing is non-destructive and temporary, but may introduce unwanted latency when recording live musicians. However, by following some simple rules and suggestions, you can use plug-ins in a live session with great results. For example, in Pro Tools, time-based processors like reverbs and delays can be used any time in the recording process, as long they are set up in a parallel connection on an aux input, and delay compensation is not applied. This is because reverbs and delays are late by nature, so having them later than normal is acceptable to our ears.

Serial plug-ins like EQs and compressors present a problem in a live session because of latency. But here's where systems such as Universal Audio's Apollo offer an elegant solution. UA's Apollo features UAD powered plug-ins, which may be applied in the record path with very low latency. By using the UA Apollo hardware, software console, and Apollo DSP, you can use any UAD serial plug-in in a live recording session without taxing your computer's internal processing power.

Another solution is to use a professional system, such as Pro Tools HD, where many Avid DSP plug-ins do not require additional delay compensation above what the system has already buffered. Pro Tools clip-based processing is an example. While some plug-ins can't be used while recording, clip-based processing can be applied to existing clips in a live session in real-time by selecting the clips, then applying EQ, compression, and more.

EQ AND COMPRESSION

The two most common processors used in music production are EQs and compressors. As you know, EQs are found on car radios, guitar amps, portable music players, and more. But there are differences between equalizers found on consumer devices and those used in professional audio production. Professional EQs cater to higher-end workflows where precision and great sound are important, so there are more features, and the signal path is of higher quality.

For example, rather than having just bass and treble controls, a pro audio EQ may have sweepable frequencies, gain, and Q controls for altering bandwidth—the bell-shaped area to the left and right of a chosen frequency. This is called a parametric EQ and can be found in hardware and plug-in processors from a variety of manufacturers.

Let's look at the Avid EQ III plug-in, found in every Pro Tools system. For starters, there are two filters that reside at the ends of the range of our hearing, which is 20Hz to 20kHz. These filters are cut only, meaning you can only reduce the level starting at the chosen frequency. They're used to reduce rumble at the low end, and to cut higher frequencies where they're not needed—for instance, where you'd want to reduce cymbal leakage on an outside kick-drum mic.

The EQ III also features five parametric bands, each with controls for boosting and cutting gain, setting the desired frequency, and adjusting the Q, which is the width of the area you are boosting or cutting. Each of the five bands represents a slice of the audible spectrum. Two extra controls found on the highest and lowest bands switch between shelf or bell, giving you even more sonic choices when EQing tracks.

A professional EQ taken to its limits of tone variance, volume, and band isolation will allow you to sonically sculpt a single track or group of tracks. Plug-ins also have the ability to add extra features beyond the basics. For example, the Drum Leveler compressor and Surfer EQ from Sound Radix give you the ability to EQ in the traditional way, but also use pitch recognition to "surf" to the area where the strongest frequencies reside.

The frequency of the upright bass is a moving target, but the Surfer accurately moves the EQ to where it's needed at the time. Keep in mind, EQ can be overused, but when tastefully applied, it helps blend the individual elements in a mix to the perfect proportions.

A compressor is a device designed to reduce the dynamic range of a signal, bringing the softest and loudest parts of the signal closer together. Common parameters include threshold, attack, ratio, release, and makeup gain.

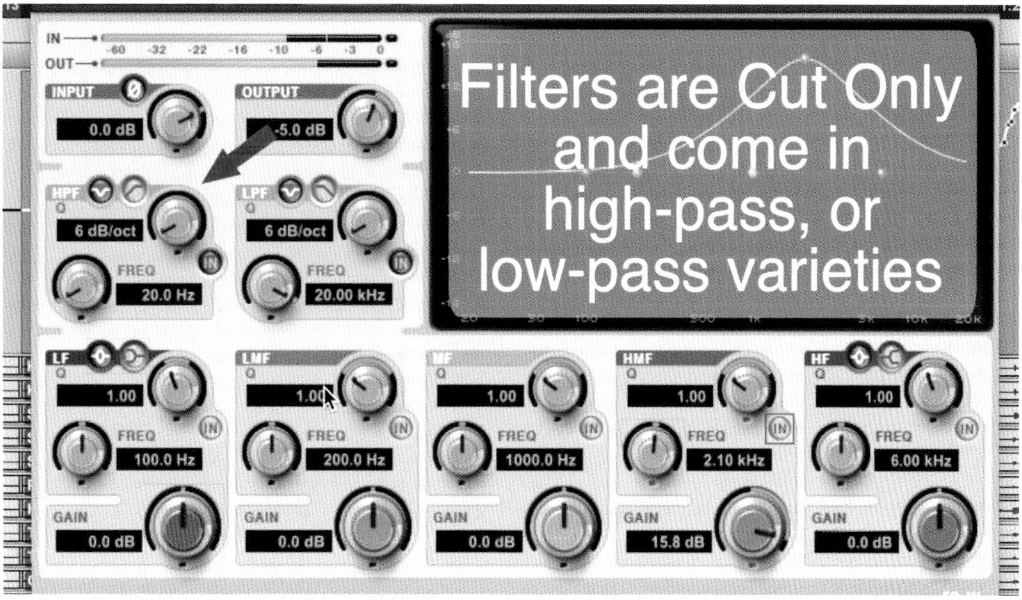

Let's dig down into how a compressor works by first understanding the dynamics of an audio signal. The envelope of a signal maps how a sound develops over time. The components of the envelope are the attack, decay, sustain, and release of the signal, or ADSR. Attack is how fast sound develops from zero to its highest peak, also known as a transient peak. Next is decay, or how the sound is reduced after the attack. Then comes sustain, or how the sound holds its energy before it finally fades which is called the release. Each of these four elements may happen quickly or slowly depending on the sound. For example, the sound of a snare drum would have a quick ADSR with fast attack transients, fast decay, very little sustain, and a quick release, whereas the sound of a bass guitar would have a fast attack, a longer decay and sustain, and a quick release, or a mix of different variations.

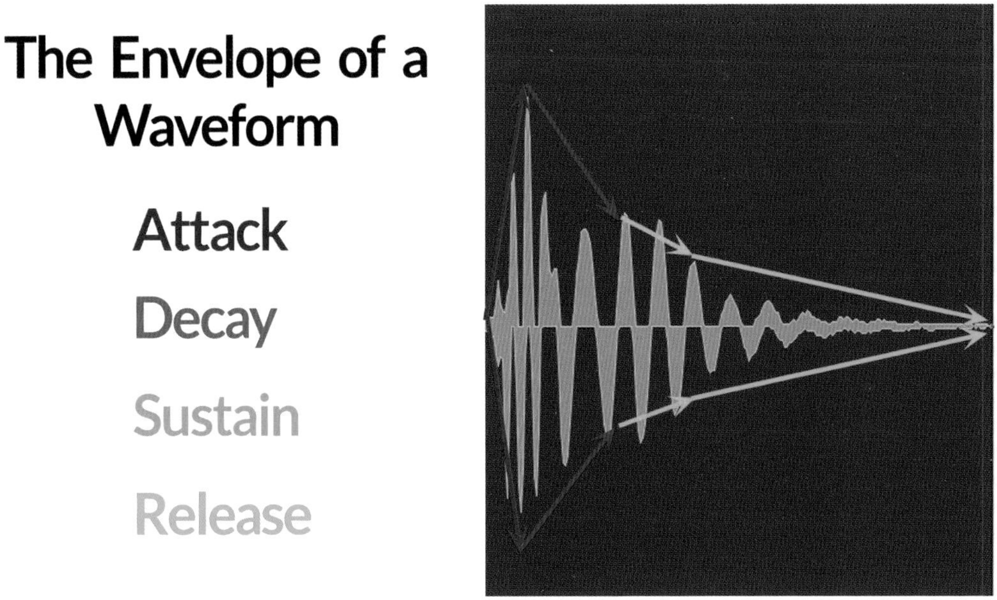

Common compressor controls define how the compressor responds to the envelope of a sound. For example, the threshold sets the level where the compressor starts reducing gain. Signal below the threshold remains untouched while signal above the threshold is reduced. Meters on the compressor or DAW give you visual feedback on the input, output, and amount of gain reduction occurring as you set the controls.

Other controls called attack and knee set how fast the compressor grabs the signal once it crosses the threshold. When set to a slow attack and soft knee, the compressor waits a specific time before it starts compressing, then gradually starts compressing the signal. Fast attack and hard knee settings would start the compression sooner, applying it immediately after the threshold is crossed.

While the attack sets timing, the compressor's ratio setting sets the *amount* of compression applied above the threshold. For example, at a 1-to-1 ratio, no compression occurs. At 4-to-1, the compressor gives back one decibel for every 4 dB above the threshold, and so on. You can also think of these relationships as fractions by turning the ratio upside down. For example, at 2-to-1, you're getting one half of the signal back in dB when it crosses the threshold. At 5-to-1, you get ⅕th back, 10-to-1, ⅒th back, and so on.

A limiter is just a compressor with a high ratio, generally 20-to-1 and up. It is also called a brick wall limiter because once the signal crosses the threshold it can get no louder.

Like the many varieties of EQs, preamps, and other gear we've discussed throughout the book, each compressor sounds different and is used for different applications. Compression can be subtle or heavy handed. And depending on the desired outcome, each approach may work to make the track better. It's all a matter of practice, taste, and preference.

TIME-BASED PROCESSING

The two most common types of time-based processors are reverb and delay. They are called time based because they lengthen a signal's envelope with digital processing. To understand a reverb, it's best to think about the space it's emulating. Is the reverb time small and reflective like a bathroom, or large and diffuse like a concert hall? How far is the listener from the source? How many early and late reflections are in the room? All these questions can be answered by adjusting the reverb parameters, which on a plug-in are found on the GUI, or graphic user interface.

For example,

- The decay time sets the length of reverb
- Pre-delay adjusts the gap in time before the reverb starts
- Diffusion simulates obstructions and other surfaces in the room
- Room size simulates the size of the space in meters

Other reverbs, like Altiverb from Audio Ease, are very sophisticated, giving you the option of using real ambience captured from an actual space. The Altiverb team regularly captures these impulse responses from select concert halls, cathedrals, stadiums, and more, as well as cherished hardware reverb units used in studios worldwide. Reverb plug-ins from a growing list of manufacturers offer a nearly endless variety of time-based effects to add to your sessions.

A delay is generally simpler than a reverb. It duplicates a sound once or many times, then adding it back to the original signal. Common controls are delay time, measured in milliseconds, feedback for adding more than a single repeat, and filtering for changing the timbre of the delays relative to the original signal. You can use delays to make a track sound thicker, or more full by setting the delay time to a smaller number, usually around 40 milliseconds. The effect can be adjusted by increasing, or decreasing the delay time.

Plug-ins can be simple processors, model tape delays, or offer other more intricate features, like Echoboy from Soundtoys. Echoboy offers more complex presets broken down by type, instrument, and voice categories to use as a starting point if you want to audition different sounds when using this versatile time-based processor.

SERIAL VS. PARALLEL PROCESSING

Once you decide on which EQ, compressor, or time-based processor to use in your production, it's important to know the best way to set it up. This is where console- and DAW-based productions use the same methods: you can either set up your device in a serial or parallel connection. A serial connection sends 100% of your signal through a processor, whereas a parallel connection sends a copy of your source signal directly to another channel, which in turn feeds the processor. Unlike a serial connection, which takes place on a single channel, a parallel connection creates a wet/dry relationship between two or more channels. This means you can separately mix your original, or dry signal, with the processed, or wet signal. Additionally, other source tracks can be sent to the same effect. There are advantages to both techniques depending on the application.

A serial processor is instanced on a single mono or stereo track. No other tracks may access this processor. EQ and compressor plug-ins are often used this way because you may not want to share them between tracks. This is because processing is not "one-size-fits-all"—an EQ that you'd use on a bass, would not be the same as you'd use on percussion. Although it is preferable to use certain kinds of processors this way, when using plug-ins, it's not an efficient use of DSP.

As we discussed in previous lessons, DSP is a finite resource, and if too many live plug-ins are used in a session, you could run out. This is where some DAWs come to the rescue, allowing you to commit or freeze your plug-in, which frees up DSP for use elsewhere. Although committing and freezing is not permanent, it does take time to do, then undo. Ideally, you'd have as much DSP as you'd need for any type of session, but because of the cost, it is not always practical. This is where setting up parallel processing for time-based processors can help save DSP. For example, the four vocal tracks here are all sent along the VOC VERB bus to a parallel auxiliary channel where the reverb resides. The source track's sends, seen on the small faders, can be panned in stereo, which will add to the width of the vocals in the mix. Because the reverb and vocal source tracks are on separate faders, they can be blended and made more dynamic as the song progresses. You could add more reverb in the choruses of the song and less in the verses. Setting up effects in parallel gives you many ways to dynamically move elements in your mix.

You can also use EQs or compressors in parallel. For instance, selected drums here are sent along a common "crush" bus to a stereo aux input where Sound Radix Drum Leveler resides. A preset can be used for quick results, which can then be fine-tuned. This is called parallel compression where the "dry" original tracks are blended with the "wet" compressed tracks to add presence. Parallel compression is not limited to drums and can be used on other mix elements as well.

If you're using a console and analog processors, it's the same scenario. You would patch your serial connections using a channel insert, and your parallel connections using an aux send. Learning how to properly set up and use serial and parallel processors can take your productions to the next level. And that's what is most important!

By learning the basics, practicing, networking with other engineers, musicians, and producers, you'll become better at the craft of making music.

Conclusion

Thank you for choosing *The Blackbird Academy Foundations* as the launching pad for your career as a music creator.

One of the key concepts when learning anything new is repetition. After going through the chapters, it's important to revisit the subject again from time to time to better integrate the concepts into your recording workflow.

As you learn, if you aren't pleased with the tracks you're recording, refer back to the signal chain. This includes the instrument, player, microphone, cable, converter, digital audio workstation, and speakers. Your recording is only as strong as your weakest link.

Compare your tracks to your favorite records, collaborate with friends, and experiment using the concepts in the chapters. It may be slow at first, but you will progress as you learn to critically listen, record, compare, and learn from your mistakes. Thanks, and congratulations on making the decision to move forward in your love for music and audio production.

About the Author

Kevin Becka has been a recording engineer for over twenty-five years, working with the top names in music, including Kenny G., Quincy Jones, Michael Bolton, George Benson, George Lynch, and more. An experienced educator, Becka is currently the co-director and instructor at the Blackbird Academy in Nashville. He has also taught advanced recording at Belmont University, taught surround recording and lectured at the Danish Rhythmic Music Conservatory in Copenhagen, Denmark, and was director of education and an instructor at the Conservatory of Recording Arts and Sciences for ten years. He is also an audio journalist who has worked as the editor of *Pro Audio Review* and *Audio Media USA* magazines. Since 2003, Becka has been the technical editor of the industry-leading Mix magazine where he writes features, product reviews, and a monthly column. He is a voting member of the National Academy of Recording Arts and Sciences (NARAS), the Country Music Association (CMA), and is a member of the American Society of Composers, Authors, and Publishers (ASCAP).